To
Best wishes
enjoy the read.
From Henry Roux

Olympic Dream
Henry Rono

authorHouse

AuthorHouse™
1663 Liberty Drive, Suite 200
Bloomington, IN 47403
www.authorhouse.com
Phone: 1-800-839-8640

© *2010 Henry Rono. All rights reserved.*

No part of this book may be reproduced, stored in a retrieval system, or transmitted by any means without the written permission of the author.

First published by AuthorHouse 10/18/2010

ISBN: 978-1-4343-2787-1 (sc)
ISBN: 978-1-4343-9170-4 (hc)

Library of Congress Control Number: 2007906026

Printed in the United States of America
Bloomington, Indiana

This book is printed on acid-free paper.

Returning to Kenya following the 1978 Commonwealth Games.

ACKNOWLEDGEMENTS

I want to express my appreciation for the people who inspired me throughout my journey in writing this book. Without their help, my book could not have been completed. The arduous process to produce a manuscript takes the organization of many minds.

In many ways, it was easier to live these 29 chapters than it was to put them in black and white on paper. Therefore, my first thanks must go to two English tutors at Central New Mexico Community College, Richard Roark and Nancy Fong. These editors have seen me through most of my schoolwork. They were diligent and thorough readers of my manuscript who helped me convey my life story with greater clarity and grace. These editors gave me the courage to relate my story and polished and examined the manuscript countless times before it reached this final draft. However, the editor who worked hardest and closest with me on this project was Tomás Radcliffe. He made this story come alive and was a friend in every step of the process. To him and his wife, Erin, who helped put the finishing touches on the text before it was sent to my publisher, I am extremely grateful.

I am also fortunate to have had the opportunity to work with Felicia Montoya and Andy Yelenak. These two artists did a remarkable job enhancing the photos I have collected over the past 29 years, altering them to not only make them publishable, but to make each an attractive work of art in its own right.

I would also like to acknowledge the people who counseled me and helped me put my life back on the right path. Tracy Sundlun was a great influence in my life and introduced me to the secretary of IAAF, John Holt, who believed in me and helped me when I was wrongly accused of a crime. I am also grateful to the president of the IAAF, Primo Nebiolo, who encouraged me to apply the same discipline I had for training my body to developing my mind. As a result of his encouragement, I pursued an education and developed the writing skills necessary to complete this book. I cannot adequately express my appreciation for the work they did for me. The doctors and counselors in various rehabilitation programs in New Jersey and Pennsylvania (USA) between 1986 and 1993 were both encouraging and inspiring. Many of the lessons I have learned about life have come from these counselors.

I thank my coach at Washington State, John Chaplin. Though we had our misunderstandings and conflicts, in retrospect, I am thankful for his efforts to help me adapt to college life in America. Coming from a small, poor village in Kenya's Rift Valley, where my family had never been exposed to an industrialized nation like America, was not an easy task for me. Without his motivation and encouragement, I would not have made it.

Most of all, I want to dedicate this book to my family, beginning with my mother, Chemaiyo, daughter of Kobotkimisik (who was born in 1890 and is still alive at the completion of this manuscript in 2007). I also dedicate this book to my son Nixon Kipngetich, who was born in September 8, 1980 and died in 1984 of cancer, as well as to my daughter, Maureen Jepchumba, and son, Calvin Kipkorir.

Finally, I thank my wife, Jennifer Jepkemboi, who endured the drastic fluctuations of my life, both on and off the track. She has celebrated my victories with me and suffered my losses, and I am blessed to have her spirit running always beside me.

FOREWORD
LEGENDS NEVER DIE

Twenty-nine years ago, the Kenyan long-distance runner Henry Rono broke four world records in 81 days, running to immortality in the 3,000 meters, 3,000 meters steeplechase, 5,000 meters, and 10,000 meters. Such a prodigious streak of world record running had never occurred before and has not happened since. It was the first time that one person held all the long-distance world records simultaneously. Two of those records stood for over a decade. No other running prodigy in history achieved such a breadth of accomplishment in such a short span of time. Henry's record-breaking streak signaled a big change in track and field. Since then, African runners have continuously improved, achieving their current superiority in the sport.

I was born in 1971, and I was too young to follow Henry's assault on track-and-field history. But later on, I always felt that there was something special about Henry Rono—people were fascinated by him, and, when I was a boy, many people told "mythic" anecdotes about this great man. This is why I was so excited the first time that I met Henry in Albuquerque, New Mexico (USA), 20 years after his incredible series of world records. I was in high-altitude training camp, and, in the evening, I met coaching legend Jama Aden (among other greats, he coached Somalian runner Abdi Bile, the 1,500-meter world champion in 1987). I entered my apartment, and suddenly Jama said, "Do you know this man, brother?" And there he was, sitting in an armchair, with his eyes lightening.

Henry Rono was then a man of almost 50 years, and his serenity and wisdom were an aura that spread throughout the room. He was the complete opposite of the image the journalists had painted of a "fallen champion." (A genius needs passion, which requires both asceticism and excesses. Henry Rono was a genius on the track, and his excesses with alcohol after his career ended brought him back into the public eye, with journalists focusing on his personal problems). In that apartment that day was a man sitting in front of me who passed gracefully through both the good and bad fortunes in his life. He remained humble through his victories, and his hardships made him stronger.

Today, Henry is a high school teacher in Albuquerque, and he has an incredible energy inside him. Before work, just for pure pleasure and exhilaration, he often goes for a 4:00 A.M. run. After work, he coaches students and amateurs, as well as world-class athletes. He tends to his own home page on the Internet, from which he responds to email inquiries immediately. Henry publishes articles and writes poems. He built a house in Albuquerque. On the weekends, he practices with his athletes in training programs in the thin air of the Sandia Mountains east of Albuquerque. This man is burning to give his knowledge and experience to young people. The fire in Henry is still as bright as it was in the summer of 1978.

Henry had—and still has—what is missing in most athletes and what is necessary for a true champion: an intense drive to compete that does not detract from his charismatic aura. Henry Rono was one of the first Africans in the 1970s to compete in Europe and North America. He was a pioneer and an inspiration for the other African runners who followed his example. Unlike contemporary Kenyan track stars, Henry didn't have a manager, a coach, or sponsor. Even under those conditions, he made his way: from a high jumper in the Nandi Hills of Kenya's Rift Valley to become the most successful sportsman in the world in 1978.

Today, there is a general void of larger-than-life champions in the track and field world. Running associations in Kenya are now affiliated with military and government organizations, and Kenyan runners are mostly managed by Europeans. Because of pioneers like Henry Rono, multinational sports companies now invest millions of dollars in Kenyan athletes and training camps in Kenya, and the best of these athletes dominate the international track meets. During the last 27 years, even the amateur sports have developed into a part of the worldwide entertainment industry. Champions who have the personality to match their athletic exploits are missing in today's world of track and field. Henry Rono was one of these rare charismatic champions. As Henry says, "We had a lot of fun together in the good old days… I'm missing that in the athletes today."

Through long runs in the Gilgi Hills of Kenya, Henry Rono forged the basis of the basic endurance he later built his legend upon. By the principles of his basic training system, with its emphasis on easy running in the thin air of the mountains on small tracks, his legs developed incredibly strong endurance. The structure of his training was simple, yet, when you ask famous sport scientists like the ones at the University of Cologne what the best way to improve endurance is, they recommend a concept that Henry Rono developed 28 years ago. All Henry needed to foster his genius was a pair of running shoes and a life that is equal parts running and contemplation.

Today, Henry Rono wants to share his experience with other people. I followed the advice he gave me in the spring of 2000, and it's no coincidence that, only a few weeks later, I won the German Championship with greater ease than I had ever won a race. In 2000 and 2001, I participated in some Rono programs with the world-class triathlete and iron man, Lothar, who specialized in long-distances. Suddenly, after following Henry's regimen, he began winning many of his competitions in the short distance as well, becoming the only triathlete of his time who was world-class in both long and short distances.

However, world-class athletes are not the only ones who can benefit from Henry's wisdom. Henry hopes to help others through his teaching career and possibly even coaching on the university level. I am convinced that Henry would be a world-class coach just as he was a world-class runner and is a world-class human being. And if he realizes his dream of coaching at the highest levels of track and field, I am convinced that his students' performances on the track will only be overshadowed by the strengthening of their character off the track.

—*Thorsten Naumann*

Chapter I
Nandi Upbringing

I was born in 1952 in Kiptaragon, a village nestled in the Nandi Hills of Kenya's Rift Valley, where long grasses cover the forest floor and where, though it doesn't rain often, when it does, it rains heavily. When I was a young boy, as the other children were running into the fields, hills, and forests to play, my only dream was to regain my ability to walk.

When I was two, my uncle was bicycling me from my grandmother's house in Turbo back to Kiptaragon when I fell from the bike, and my right leg slid into the wheel spoke and snapped at the ankle. For many years, as other children my age grew stronger and faster, I was only able to crawl. I remember my mother constantly asking herself and others, "Will he ever be able to walk again?"

This accident was one of many incidents—which others might deem unfortunate—that I had to overcome to become a world-class runner. And, while a few of the better known of these incidents may have interfered with my chances to run in the Olympics, I do not consider these incidents misfortunes. After all, they have shaped me as a human being, making me stronger both emotionally and intellectually. In the end, it was, I believe, my psychological toughness, tempered by the many obstacles I had to overcome in my early life and young adulthood, that made me a superior middle-distance runner.

By the late 1950s, when I was about six years old, I was finally able to walk again. However, around this time, I experienced what would be one of the most devastating setbacks of my life. My father was working on a tractor on a farm owned by a White man when a snake rose up in front of the tractor's front wheel and startled him. He jumped back from the tractor and landed on a three-disc plough. He died instantly.

My father's death came at a critical juncture in my upbringing. In Nandi culture, boys are raised primarily by their mothers, who teach them basic skills and values, until they are six years old. At the age of six, a boy's father begins to play a more prominent role in raising him and teaching him how to become a man. By the time a Nandi boy is 10, he is expected to assume a man's responsibilities, which consist mostly of outdoor work, from hunting and working in the fields to looking after animals. Because my father died at the very time he would have begun to assert more influence over my life, my mother and grandmother had to fill dual roles in my upbringing, offering not only maternal guidance, but becoming father figures to me as well. Fortunately for me, they were both strong women. My mother was raised by a Nandi warrior who was forced by the British to fight and die in World War I. My grandmother, whom I call Kobotkimisik, is perhaps the strongest woman I know, and her strength is attested to by her longevity: she was born in 1890 and, unbelievably, is still alive today. My grandfather, Kibutuut Arap Maswai, was recruited to serve in World War I as part of the Third Battalion King's African Rifles led by Lieutenant Colonel Paul Von Lettow-Vorbeck when war broke out in August 1914. My grandfather was one of the 12,00 African soldiers or Askari who served in World War I, most of whom would never return.

Many of my fondest memories from childhood are of my grandmother telling me bedtime stories about the history and traditions of our Nandi ancestors. She told me how the Nandis immigrated to the hills of the Rift Valley from along the Nile River in Egypt. She told me how the Nandi tribes resisted British colonialism since the first expeditions of White explorers came through Kenya during the 19th century. In the late 19th century and during the first half of the 20th century, as other African tribes quickly submitted to British rule, the Nandi retained much of their land and independence.

My grandmother also told me of the Nandi prophet Orkoiyot Koitalel Arap Samoei, who received visions warning of the arrival of the White man's exploitative industries. One of Samoei's most frightening visions was of a long snake that released fire and dark smoke into the air from its tail. When the British colonists arrived in the Rift Valley, the Nandis realized that Samoei's vision was a prophecy of the White man's trains, which would bring destruction to their land and disrupt their tribal way of life. Realizing the symbolic significance of Samoei's vision, the Nandi opposed colonization from the beginning, and wherever railroad tracks were laid, Nandis ripped them from the ground and used the wood and metal to make arrows and spears with which to fend off the British. Though the British had rifles, the tenacity of the Nandi resistance, combined with the natural barriers of the landscape of the Rift Valley, with its hills, basins, and forests, thwarted all early British military attempts to colonize the Nandis.

While aggressive attempts to colonize my ancestors failed, the spirit of the Nandi people fell after the assassination of Samoei in 1905. Many lost direction and became victims of alcoholism. I remember my grandmother saying, "If not for the man who killed our prophet, we would still have fresh air to breathe in joy and peace."

Because of the general feeling of pessimism and the prevalence of alcohol addiction in Nandi villages after the establishment of British rule, more and more Nandis began to embrace some aspects of Western culture, especially Christianity, with its emphasis on Western education. Catholic missionaries attempted to bridge the gap between Nandi beliefs and Christian doctrine, and they were able to attract many Nandis to their religion, as well as to Western values in general, by offering athletic programs for Nandi youth. However, while Western and Christian influences became increasingly integrated into Nandi culture, it is important to emphasize two points: first, compared to other tribes in the region who were quickly overpowered by the British, the Nandis were slow to embrace Western and Christian values, and, second, at least through the first half of the 20th century, the parts of Western and Christian culture that the Nandis did embrace generally did not overshadow or diminish their own tribal beliefs and values. Therefore, many Nandis who practiced Christianity also continued to practice ancient Nandi rituals, such as the extraction of the bottom front two teeth and circumcision for boys and girls as preparation for adulthood and marriage.

For the most part, my family was not heavily exposed to Western culture until the early 1960s, when I began attending school and going to church services. Still, during this period, my mother encouraged me to put my Nandi heritage before school and Christianity, and so I had my bottom front two teeth extracted when I was 10 years old.

Because my knowledge of Nandi culture is due in large part to my grandmother's storytelling, as well as the songs I grew up singing about Samoei and other Nandi warriors, perhaps the best way to relate my experience of the Nandi tooth ritual, as well as the precedence my tribal upbringing took over school and Christianity, is through a poem I wrote in for a creative writing class in 2005:

Nandi Rituals

"Get up and get ready to go to the Nandi tooth ritual,"
Mother said.
I was in elementary school.

My two bottom front teeth were pulled out
Without painkillers
On a Sunday morning.

I thought of going to church.

It was not an option that morning.

"The Nandi rituals come first today," said Mother.

I told Hut Man that Mother said to take out the two teeth

From my jaw and from my sister's.

I bit on wood across my mouth.

The sharp arrow plate slashed through my gums.

The two teeth were pulled out and fell on my lap.

I picked them up and threw them straight to the sky

And asked the sun to take these two teeth away and give me
    wishes for a new life!

The blood dripped down my chest.

They handed me a huge jug of milk, with cheers for a good
    boy who never cries!

I drank it up until it was empty.

On returning home, I told Mother about the tooth

And school connection.

She said, "You gave away your two teeth today.

Your circumcision will be next.

After that, you will be a man and ready to get married."

At the time I took part in the tooth ritual in 1962, many Nandis were beginning to conform to Western ideals to the exclusion of their tribal customs. In fact, by the early 1960s, so many Nandi children who were attending school or church had given up tribal rituals that, when I arrived at the ritual leader's hut to have my teeth pulled, he expressed surprise, saying, "I thought you just started going to school. You will not be able to speak good English because the air will go through there." I simply responded, "Mother wants me to be a good Nandi." The ritual leader's skepticism was a sign of things to come in the second half of the 20th century, as many Nandis found it increasingly difficult to reconcile their tribal heritage with Western culture and Christianity.

The tension between Western values and Nandi culture in the 1960s was prefaced by the great political upheaval in Kenya during the 1950s. The year I was born, Jomo Kenyatta was jailed for allegedly inciting a violent uprising against British rule. Seven years later, around the time I was learning to walk again, he was released from prison. In the 1963 election, I remember my mother saying she had cast her vote for Jomo, and, in June of that year, he became Kenya's Prime Minister.

Under Kenyatta's leadership in 1964, the new government declared the free education act for single parents, and I was hopeful that this would allow me to get my Certificate of Primary Education

(CPE) without bringing financial hardship on my family. When my mother became a widow years earlier, she was unable to pay for school fees, so, once I was able to walk again, I began working for my neighbor as a herd boy, making five shillings a month until the government began harassing my mother about my not attending school. I remember thinking to myself at that time, "We barely have enough to eat, so where would my mother find the money for school fees and uniforms?"

My mother was able to raise enough money selling home brews of *chang'aa* a*nd busaa*, two very potent alcoholic concoctions, to pay for the school fees. Soon, I was attending Kabirirsang Primary School, where, newly limp-free, I became a star midfielder on the soccer team. Though things seemed to be going well with my education, the school fees were still hard to afford, and, some months, my mother wasn't sure whether she would be able to pay them. While the free education act for single parents seemed like a godsend to my mother and me, the new act proved meaningless as corrupt officials took advantage of poor people, demanding ever more exorbitant fees because they knew no one in the new government would do anything to stop it.

"She will pay like any other parent. If not, we will confiscate her property, which is one of her cows," said the head of the school council who married my mother's younger sister and refused to accept my five shillings. They wanted my mother to pay 70 shillings, which was an absurdly high price for a poor, single mother.

    To help offset these rising debts, my mother had my older sister circumcised and married her off to a Kenyan army soldier for a dowry of five cows, five sheep, two goats, and 500 Kenyan shillings, which was enough to pay for my primary education almost until the time of my CPE examination. At this point, with my family running out of money from the dowry, I began working for the Nandi Tea Estate and used the money I earned there to pay for my last year of school. While plowing the fields of the tea estate, other workers would look out over the village and say, "You see that smoky house down there? I heard they made a good one yesterday." The house they were referring to was my mother's, and the smoke was from her brewing *chang'aa* a*nd busaa*. Vagrants and drunks would gather around my mother's house, and, whenever an especially potent brew was made, they were sure to pass along the word, which evidently would reach as far as the tea estate by noon. I was ashamed to tell them that the house was my mother's, even though I was proud of her for swallowing her pride and doing whatever it took to in order make ends meet for our family.

    The combination of idealism and ineffectiveness exemplified by the free education act for single parents is symbolic of the overall leadership of Jomo Kenyatta's administration. While Kenyatta is often referred as the father of Kenyan nationalism and revered for leading native Kenyans to independence, his reforms often failed to live up to their initial promise and were susceptible to corruption. While the single parent education act promised my mother education for her children at no cost, the reality was that she ended up paying much more than she previously had for my school fees to corrupt officials. Similarly, though Kenyatta preached Kenyan independence, he allowed British officials to retain influence in the government and pushed for many Western-influenced reforms that were dependent upon the continued presence of British troops. Kenyatta also received much criticism for favoring his own tribe, the Kikuyu, especially in regards to land reform. Today, Kenyatta remains both a revered and controversial figure in Kenya. However, politics aside, compared to his successor, he was encouraging of my running career and, just before he died in the 1978, he embraced me for the world records I had broken, honoring me as a national hero. Nonetheless, it should be noted that he was often neglectful of the needs of his athletes and allowed his star runners to be used by Kenyan Amateur Athletic Association (KAAA) officials as political pawns.

Kenyatta's death in 1978 signaled the beginning of a tumultuous time in Kenyan politics. Beyond this, the 1980s, under the rule of Daniel arap Moi, were an era of much oppression in general, including a great deal of hostility toward track athletes who had left Kenya to attend universities or compete abroad.

CHAPTER II
The Inspiration of Kip Keino

In 1968, the Kenyan runner Kip Keino beat the American hero, Jim Ryun, in the 1,500 meters at the Mexico City Olympics. I heard the news on the radio that evening at my home in Kiptaragon Village. The victory was like a thunderclap, and all of Kenya was stunned into silence. It was at this moment that I decided to give up soccer and become a distance runner. Kip Keino became the main topic of discussion among my peers at Kabirirsang Primary School as my friends and I challenged each another to become the next Kip Keino.

In 1971, Kip Keino gave a speech to inspire young athletes at a sports stadium not far from where I lived. I attended the speech with the intention of studying his appearance and how he carried himself. The local politicians honored and welcomed him, and there was a big crowd waiting for him at the stadium. When Kip Keino arrived, the speaker asked him to raise his hand so that the crowd could see him. After the ceremony, I was so excited and inspired that I ran the entire eight miles back home from the ceremony, truly believing that someday I would be the best runner in the world. At this point, I realized that if I was going to take the next step and make my dream a reality, I would have to join the Kenyan Army, which recruited the most promising Kenyan runners and provided them with a sanctuary for training.

When I arrived at the military campus in 1973, 80% of my service consisted of running, which was, in my opinion, less tedious and rigorous than the traditional military activities of normal servicemen. The training at the Kenyan Army facilities was basic and no-nonsense, and yet it was the first formal training I had received. Up until this point, I had been a self-made runner, integrating my conversations with athletes I encountered around my village into my training regimen. While the advice I received in the army was valuable, I was still able to retain a sense of independence and self-sufficiency in regards to my training as I was encouraged to evaluate my own progress as a runner and alter my exertion accordingly.

In truth, I believe the reason for the meteoric improvements in my running during my time in the Kenyan Army had more to do with the environment than the coaching I received. My endurance improved greatly from running the steep incline of the Gilgil Hills that rose above the army barracks and strengthened my legs and will, while the elevation of these hills, which approached 7,000 feet above sea level, increased my lung capacity. I had two hills to train on every day: one for the early morning run, called Mama Ngina Hills, and the other for the afternoon run, named Taifa (Nation) Hill. Later, it was renamed Rono Hill and has since become the training ground for many elite Kenyan runners.

Still, there were a number of invaluable training techniques I learned from coaches during my army years that were formative to my running style and technique. One such training method, which is now much more common among elite athletes, is the Fartlek workout. This workout is a form of interval training for groups of runners in which the elite runners break away from the pack until a coach blows his whistle, signaling them to stop and wait for the slower runners to advance. Not only does the Fartlek method improve the efficiency with which your body uses oxygen, by using elite runners to increase the pace of slower runners, it encourages team unity, friendly competition, and camaraderie—qualities I believe are drastically underemphasized in the training of American track squads at all levels.

Coach Kinyua was one person who had a profoundly positive impact upon me during my time in the Kenyan Army. He was the first person who predicted that I would break a world record, telling me that, with the rapid improvements he saw in my times over my first months in Gilgil, I was capable of breaking the world record in the 5,000 meters. I remember Kinyua telling me, "Never, ever let an opponent pass on the back straightaway or on the home straightaway. There are four turns on a track and after each your competitor will try to make his move. But keep in front of him, hug the inside lane, and be stubborn. Each time you deny another runner a pass, his spirit will sink, and upon being denied his third or fourth try to pass, he will surrender completely." Kinyua's words became gospel to me.

By early 1974, my training started producing promising results. During the National Army Championships, I bettered Olympic gold medallist Naftali Temu's long-standing Kenyan Army records in the 10,000 meters, 5,000 meters, and 3,000-meter steeplechase. My name appeared in the newspaper for the first time that summer. Then, one day, a BBC sports reporter asked team captain Franks Munene, "Kenya is losing heroes into the professional circuit: Kip Keino, Ben Jipcho, and John Kipkurgat. Who do you think will be the next hero in Kenya?"

Munene responded without hesitation, "Henry Rono." By the end of the 1974 Kenyan running season, I was selected to travel with the Kenyan national team to the East African Friendly Championship competition that was held in Uganda.

Chapter III
Kenyan National Team

One of the things about being an elite track athlete I am most grateful for was the opportunity it afforded me to visit parts of the world and cultures that a poor Nandi boy otherwise would not have had the opportunity to see. Though Jinja, Uganda was only a short bus trip from the port city of Kisumu, Kenya, the journey offered breathtaking sights like Owen Falls, which produces electric power for many African countries. While I have since had the opportunity to visit many impressive cultural landmarks and historic sites all through Europe, Asia, and the Americas, I still recall how in awe I was of Owen Falls as I had the chance to watch machinery turn water from the River Nile into electric light. The trip to Jinja also marked the first time I stayed in a fancy hotel. Still, however awestruck I was by the fancy Silver Hotel, Owen Falls, or the pure bustle of the big city, what I was most excited for during my trip to Java was the opportunity to meet one of my heroes, the Tanzanian runner Filbert Bayi. Unfortunately, the Tanzanian team didn't show up as the team was prohibited to run due to Idi Amin's standing with Tanzania at the time. This incident served as my first introduction to the ways in which political disputes can impinge upon an athlete's career.

The trip to Jinja also served as my introduction to how poorly many African nations took care of their elite runners. Though we stayed in a nice hotel, the rest of the accommodations our team received were measly. After team manager and Kenyan hero Ben Jipcho checked our squad into the hotel, we all went out for supper. I thought we were going to be served decent meals, but the plates we received were the size of very small appetizers. I had a bowl of rice, watery soup, and a cup of tea—that was it. It went down my throat very fast, and I was prepared for more, but it turned out that was all they had. From my hotel room, I could see military personnel coming in and out of that hotel frequently. In the parking lot was a Mercedes Benz full of Idi Amin's soldiers: Idi Amin must have run the Ugandan economy dry to a point where they couldn't afford enough meals for visitors! After dinner, everyone on the team was saying, "Was that all?" and we all started rolling our eyes. During the week I was in Jinja, though my stomach was always empty, my running performance was strong. I returned to Kenya as a well-known running phenom.

In 1975, I had a trial for the New Zealand games in Mombassa, which is on the southeastern coast of Kenya on the Indian Ocean, and I won the 5,000 meters, earning a place on the Kenyan team that would travel to New Zealand. The trip would mark the first time I realized that I could compete against White people. It was also my first plane trip. It took 28 hours to travel from Nairobi to New Zealand, and, when we arrived, I was exhausted for days before I adjusted to the time change. During my first days of training in New Zealand, it felt like my body was still asleep when I was running. I was able to race on a pre-trial 3,000 meters flat competition with the Tanzanian hero, Filbert Bayi. It was a blustery, rainy day and, despite the poor weather, Bayi and I pulled away from the pack, setting a remarkable pace. Bayi beat me with the time of 7:52. I finished just seconds behind him, and the audience applauded me enthusiastically, amazed to see me not only keep up with the blistering pace of the Tanzanian hero, but to do so in such stormy weather.

The following day, the New Zealand games began. My first race was the 5,000 meters in a field that included New Zealander and record holder Dick Quix. I finished third. The following day, I ran the 3,000 meter steeplechase and came in second. The last day of the meet, I ran the 10,000 meters and finished second once again. Though I had little experience in international competitions, I was already proving my ability to contend with the world's elite runners. I overheard my teammates whispering to one another, "He is like Kip Keino. He is going to be the next hero in Kenya."

After the New Zealand games, I went to another meet in Australia before heading back to Kenya. In Australia, I ran the 5,000 meters unchallenged. During the banquet, I was able to meet the Australian hero, Ron Clark, who used to be a rival of my hero, Kip Keino, in the 1960s. When we were ready to head back to Kenya, we could not fly across the Indian Ocean due to an intense monsoon wind, which we were told would break the plane into pieces. When I heard the news, I cried out, "Oh no! I haven't married yet!" since, in Nandi culture, men are not supposed to risk their lives until they are certain their family name will be carried on. Some of my teammates grew impatient and told the pilots that they were going to look into just taking a ship. "Are you crazy?" the pilots laughed incredulously. "It would take months to sail from Perth to Mombassa!"

While the crew of the aircraft spent days monitoring the wind and considering alternate routes across the Indian Ocean, I took advantage of the free time to do some sightseeing around Perth. My first stop was the Perth Zoo, where I became fascinated by the kangaroos and other marsupials native only to Australia. I could never have conceived of such wondrously strange animals. The way the marsupials carried their young in their pouch reminded me of how my mother, like most African mothers, carried me close to her body, virtually attached to her by an expanse of cloth. The image of my mother that the kangaroos evoked helped to ease my fear of the plane plunging nose-first into the Indian Ocean. By the time I returned from the zoo, the pilots had made up their minds to follow the direction of the wind to South Africa, where we landed in Cape Town safely.

In South Africa, we were told not to leave the airport due to South Africa's policy of apartheid. While I was in the airport hotel, I saw Black workers whose eyes and expressions wore the hopelessness of lifelong imprisonment. Pointing out of the airport hotel's window, one of the managers on the team said, "You see those islands at the far side of the ocean? That is where Nelson Mandela is jailed." At that time, Mandela had been in prison for over a dozen years for his leadership of the African National Congress. He would remain imprisoned for over 15 more years before gaining his freedom in 1990 and subsequently leading his people from apartheid to become the first democratically elected president of South Africa. When our connecting plane arrived, we hurried onto it, anxious to leave the oppressive feeling of South Africa behind, which was apparent even from our extremely limited vantage of the country.

CHAPTER IV
Never Run in Combat Boots

As soon as I got back to Kenya, I returned to my usual training routine at the Gilgil barracks, but with even greater focus and intensity so as to achieve my goal of qualifying for the 1976 Olympics in Montreal. I trained so hard that soon I had worn out all of my running shoes, and I began training in my military-issued combat boots. At the time, I rationalized that training in the heavy boots might increase my speed by making my feet seem light when I returned to using running spikes. However, beyond this rationalization was the simple fact that the boots were the only shoes I had left. After a few months, when I had become accustomed to running in the boots, I injured my right ankle, which is the same one I had injured when I was two years old.

Training in my military boots aggravated my childhood injury, and, while I received a variety of treatments for it, none proved effective. Since an X-ray revealed that I had no broken bones and because modern medical treatments hadn't worked, I decided to try traditional herbal treatments. At one point, I became so frustrated with the injury that I even approached a witch doctor because I was convinced that my ankle must be related to a psychological problem. Like they say in my tribe, when someone rises quickly to success, jealous people often witch them. At the time, I became very disturbed and emotional and let my problems on the track affect my psychological state, which even led me to struggle with my first bout with depression.

I went limping from modern doctor to native herbalist with the hope that a traditional treatment might allow me to run again. Because of my injury, I was a spectator at the 1975 Kenyan Army Championship. By the end of the season, my injuries finally subsided. I later found out that the combat boots had torn a ligament in my ankle. Once I stopped running in the boots and gave my ligament sufficient time to rest, it recovered quickly and, before long, I was back on two feet and training vigorously, trying to make up for lost time in my preparations to qualify for the 1976 Olympic Games.

In early 1976, I changed my training base from the desert hills surrounding the Gilgil barracks to the cold green forests of Nyahururu, where the elevation is the highest of any town in Kenya—between 7,000 and 8,000 feet above sea level. Not only does Nyahururu offer the advantages of high elevation and steep terrain, its temperate climate, which is noticeably cooler than nearby Gilgil's, allows athletes to train for longer durations. Because of these factors, it is an ideal training refuge frequented by many of the world's premier distance runners.

One of the most famous runners who trained in Nyahururu was Lasse Viren, who won two gold medals in the 1972 Olympics and whom I met at Thompson Falls Lodge, where he stayed while training for the 1976 Olympics. In the early mornings after my training, I could see him trotting along the road between Nyahururu and Nanyuki at a snail's pace and wondered to myself, "Is this the guy who won two gold medals in the Munich Olympics?" Being surrounded by great runners like Viren in Nyahururu allowed me to not only pick their brains about training techniques and race strategies, but also to observe their habits firsthand. The untraditional methods of some runners, like Viren's very slow, self-absorbed pace during his morning run, made me not only question many traditional training methods, but gave me the confidence I needed to trust my body and mind's lead—even if this meant doing an exceedingly slow run in which my goal is to focus my mind and relax my body rather than merely push myself toward exhaustion.

That year, I participated in all of the KAAA meets. Pekka Rinne, the Finnish reporter, and Robert Hartman, a reporter from Germany, closely monitored my performance in these events and, after my victory in one 5,000-meter race, Rinne told me that, had I been running on a Tartan track, my time would have qualified me for the Olympics. Rinne was also there to observe my performance at the National Army Cross-Country Championship, a race that followed many of the most demanding high-elevation trails in Kenya. I ran so well in the championship that Rinne wrote an article about my prospects for the upcoming Olympics, which he later told me was the longest article he had ever written about a young athlete. In the article, he said that if the KAAA would set up a competitive race program for me, I would certainly medal in Montreal; however, if they continued handling me negligently and did not provide me the proper race program, it would be impossible for even a runner of my promise to compete with elite international runners in Olympic competition. After Rinne's article was published, I began seriously questioning my ties to the KAAA for the first time.

Qualifying for the Montreal Olympics proved to be no easy task as I traveled to meets in many different countries trying to qualify. Time after time I failed. I even went as far as China, where I knew the facilities would be superior to the ones I was accustomed to in Kenya and where the stadium had a Tartan track. However, the advantages of China's excellent facilities were negated by two factors: one, I was extremely tired from the long flight and change in time, and, two, the Chinese runners were not capable of challenging me in my races. Though I won each of the races I ran during the one-day meet, the 5,000 meters, the steeplechase, and the 10,000 meters, I failed to qualify for the Olympics in any of these events.

Regardless of my failure to qualify, the trip to China would prove valuable to me as it helped wake me to the KAAA's corruption and mishandling of Kenyan athletes. The contrast was clear: even though the Chinese boast very few runners who are competitive in international competitions, their athletes are treated with respect and their athletic facilities are state-of-the-art; conversely, Kenya, which boasts many of the world's finest runners, disrespects its athletes through its governing body for athletics, the KAAA, with its domineering policies and antiquated facilities.

While the KAAA was routinely neglectful of its athletes, there were, nonetheless, a number of national team coaches who were good to me and other athletes and who looked after our needs and treated us with respect. For instance, after I had returned from China, I traveled to Zanzibar, Tanzania to compete in the East Africa Championships, where I was still trying to qualify for the Olympics. Though I failed to qualify on this trip, I certainly could not blame my failure on paltry serving sizes since coach Kip Keino, who remembered the small meals we received in Jinja, brought sacks filled with cornmeal and beans so that we would be able to cook for ourselves whenever we were hungry. As we unloaded our bags from the plane, Kip Keino, half in jest, yelled, "Don't forget the beans and cornmeal, boys!"

By the time I flew back to Kenya, I was a nervous wreck because my time to qualify for the Olympics was running out. After failing an attempt to qualify for the 3,000-meter steeplechase in a meet in Kisumu, I was told that I would have only one more chance to qualify, in Mombassa. Filbert Bayi, the Tanzanian runner who had pushed me to run an impressive 3,000-meter race the previous year in New Zealand, had traveled to Kenya to try and qualify for the Olympics in the 1,500 meters. Seeing Bayi must have inspired me as I ran the 3,000 steeplechase in an impressive 8:29, becoming the last runner to qualify for the Kenyan Olympic squad.

Chapter V
Olympic Preparations

The Olympic training camp in Kenya proved extremely demanding, offering the most stringent training regimen I had experienced up to that point in my running career. Kip Keino, the training camp director, had very strict rules for athletes and threatened to expel any runner who violated team policies. I welcomed the camp's rules as the regimen helped me to focus on my goal of becoming an Olympic medallist.

While the training camp's early morning runs were similar to the ones I did in army training, the interval workouts were much more mechanical, putting more emphasis on technique than exertion. For instance, in training for the steeplechase, I spent much of my time working on quickening my jumps so that I could save a fraction of a second on each barrier, which the coaches told me could lead to a 7-to 14-second improvement on my time over the course of the race. Once I mastered these techniques two years later, I was able to reduce my steeplechase time from the 8:29 I ran to qualify for the Montreal Olympics to a world best of 8:05.4.

Once we arrived in the Olympic Village in Montreal, Kip Keino instilled a different system of training based upon his own Olympic preparations, putting greater emphasis on mental exercises and nutritional monitoring and requiring us to retain discipline and focus even during our free time. After a few days in the Olympic Village, it became apparent why Keino's restrictions on our free time were necessary as many athletes fell prey to frivolous distractions. Some athletes on the Kenyan team treated the festive atmosphere of Montreal and the Olympic Village as if it were the end point of our journey and the main reason why we had traveled so far. These athletes embraced the nightlife and attractions, shopping and carrying on as if the celebrations and festivities were more important than the games themselves. Other athletes rested on their laurels, believing that they had already proven themselves by making the Olympic team and did not even bother to get up for early-morning workouts. A few athletes exerted their energy in battling our team's contractual obligation to our corporate sponsor, Adidas. The Kenyan Olympic team's contract with Adidas was exclusive, meaning that we were not allowed to wear any other company's shoes or apparel. However, many athletes on the team insisted on wearing Pumas, Tigers, or other brands, and the obstinacy of these individuals disrupted our team's sense of unity.

Witnessing how unfocused many of my teammates and other athletes in the Olympic Village were instilled in me a sense of quiet confidence, as I knew that my focus was pure. I was not going to squander my chance for an Olympic medal by distracting myself with frivolous issues of sponsorship rights or by partaking in any form of overconsumption, whether shopping, overeating, drinking, or partying. Kip Keino told me that it required every ounce of his focus and energy to defeat Jim Ryun in Mexico City, and I wanted to make sure that I was as prepared for my Olympic chance as my hero had been for his battle with that great American runner in 1968.

My focus and dedication in the Olympic Village began to stand out amid my peers. Kip Keino told me to prepare for an additional event, the 5,000 meters, which was a relief since, if I missed a gold medal in the steeplechase, I'd now have another opportunity to claim one. When I won both the 5,000-meter and 3,000-meter steeplechase trials, the number of compliments I received from coaches and the officials increased. I overheard one saying, "We have an athlete on the Kenyan team who promises to challenge for two

Olympic golds." The Olympics were about to start, and my mind was focused and my body perfectly tuned.

Everything changed the night before the opening ceremony, when we received word that the Kenyan team would not participate in the Olympics due to a boycott in protest of the inclusion of New Zealand, which still had athletic ties to the apartheid government of South Africa. We were told to pack our bags immediately, and we headed straight to the airport, arriving back in Kenya the next day. When the press asked for my reaction to the boycott, I wasn't sure how to respond except to say that since I was 16 years old, that I had a dream to become a great runner in the Olympics, and now, eight years later, strenuous training and strict mental discipline, I had approached the pinnacle of my dream, establishing myself as a medal contender. However, just as I was about to be given the chance to attain this dream, it was taken from me. My Olympic dream had turned into Olympic smoke rings.

While I was in the Olympic Village in Montreal, I heard talk about how foreign runners who emigrated to compete in the United States were better compensated for their talents than runners who remained in Kenya competing for the KAAA. In America, runners who competed collegiately were compensated with first-rate educations, which would help prepare them for a life and career beyond the track, while runners who turned professional were afforded the freedom to compete in whatever circuit events they chose, allowing them to tend to their own personal and monetary interests instead of being at the mercy of their country's athletic association. By the time I stepped off that plane in Kenya, I made up my mind to find a way to follow the lead of independent Kenyan runners like Mike Boit and Wilson Waigwa and defect from the Kenyan Army to escape the KAAA's oppressive handling of my career. At the times, I could not have imagined what a long, arduous, and, at time, dangerous process asserting autonomy over my running career would become.

Later, I would remember that Jonathon Nge'no, a friend of mine who happened to be working on his doctoral degree in political science in the United States, had told me about a track coach he knew from the school he was studying at, Washington State University (WSU). I asked Nge'no if he could put me in contact with this coach, whom I later learned was named John Chaplin, and he quickly obliged. Within a few weeks, Coach Chaplin had finalized my admission into WSU and sent me a plane ticket that would eventually land me in Pullman, a rural, college town located in southeastern Washington.

Chapter VI
Washington State University

I arrived in Pullman on October 1, 1976, two weeks after classes had started, and spent my first night in the United States in a motel room. The next morning, I was still groggy from my 24-hour flight when Coach Chaplin knocked on my door to introduce himself and ask me to breakfast. While we sat in the restaurant waiting for our food, Chaplin talked in a rapid stream and in an enthusiastic, but firm voice. In fact, he spoke so excitedly that sprays of saliva often accompanied his words. Although I understood some of what Chaplin was saying, he spoke too rapidly for me to pick up on more than fragments of his speech—though I gathered he was alternating between talking to me about running and welcoming me to Pullman. In addition to my inability to keep up with Chaplin's quick-paced conversation, my responses to his questions were also inhibited by my own social anxieties. I was unaccustomed to interacting with White people and was afraid to do or say something that, though culturally appropriate to me, might be offensive or distasteful to an American. When our food arrived, I was confused as to whether I should wait until I was finished chewing before responding to Chaplin's questions or whether such hesitations would be perceived as disrespectful. Since it is a great sign of disrespect in my culture to speak with one's mouth full, I decided to wait for long pauses in the conversation to take bites of my food.

As soon as we finished breakfast, we went straight to the registrar's office and picked up my student ID. On the way, Chaplin asked me about what I planned to major in. Mathematics was my response, which was more than agreeable to Chaplin since he had a friend in the math department who had expressed his admiration for Kip Keino and his interest in the history of Kenyan running. In the registrar's office, Chaplin told me, "If they ask your age, tell them you're 20." Though I was 24 at the time, I did as Chaplin told me and lied about my age.

Since the fall semester was already in its third week, Chaplin took me straight to my first class, which happened to be history. On the way to class, Chaplin and I first talked about the recent Olympic boycott and then about my prospects for the Moscow Olympics.

When we arrived at Dr. Ed Garrison's history class, Chaplin was quick to let him know that I could have won a gold medal in Montreal had Kenya not boycotted the Olympics—as if my running achievements had a direct correlation to my academic prospects. I started to suspect that Chaplin had connections with particular teachers who were willing to "go easy" on his star athletes—as if it were only natural that one's surplus athletic talent could easily compensate for any deficiencies in one's academic performance.

My fears started to deepen from the first day of history class as I began to worry about how, with my limited education, which was equivalent to the completion of the sixth- or seventh-grade level in the United States, I would be able to keep up with a college workload. Compounding my academic fears was the fact that I could hardly speak, much less write, English and that I was undergoing a severe culture shock—attempting to transition from a poor African upbringing to an almost all-White "all-American" college town. At the end of my first week of classes, I could hardly stand it anymore, but before I could confess my anxieties and doubts to Coach Chaplin in his office, he handed me $20 and introduced me to Samson Kimombwa, a fellow Kenyan who would act as my mentor, showing me the ropes and how to adjust not only to college life, but also American culture. Samson and I went to the dormitory to eat and then to a convenience store, where we used the money

Chaplin gave me to buy beer. Meeting Samson and washing down my misgivings with Budweiser after Budweiser were enough to assuage my fears for a while.

Before I arrived at WSU, running had always been a sanctuary to me. As my heart rate began rising on the track or trail, all the worries and problems I had would quickly fade away. For the most part, this remained true during my years at WSU, as the track became an escape from my homesickness and anxieties about school. Still, something about running became tarnished when I started competing for Coach Chaplin. My growing confusion and uneasiness about my relationship with Chaplin added to my anxieties. It was not merely a matter of communication, though this was certainly part of the problem, as he talked so fast that I usually had difficulty understanding what he was saying. (I would later learn that people often referred to him as "motor mouth.") No, my main issue with Chaplin was the aggressiveness, even hostility, of his coaching style. Chaplin often yelled at his runners, cursed at and threatened them, and used foul language, and he was particularly hostile and vulgar to his Kenyan runners.

To give Chaplin the benefit of the doubt, perhaps some of his words and actions on the track or in the locker room were just part of his coaching persona. And perhaps some of what I deemed most offensive was just part of the usual irreverent banter that—

however insensitive or derogatory it would appear within the public domain—passes as acceptable within the ultra-macho environment of an American university's locker room or athletic field. Still, even if this were the case, Chaplin should have been more sensitive to the cultural differences of his African athletes and made an attempt not to offend their values and sensibilities. Beyond this, I must emphasize that there were certain aspects of his coaching style, as well as certain things he said to me personally, that were inexcusable and can only be perceived as racist. For example, one afternoon, when a number of us Kenyans runners were meeting with Coach Chaplin in his office, he asked us whether we had ever groped a woman like Americans do, kissing and touching her in every private place. Chaplin told us that if we hadn't, then something was wrong with us. "You Kenyans are primates," he said, "You don't know what you are missing."

On many different occasions, when a Kenyan runner did not perform well in a race, Chaplin would threaten to have him deported if he didn't improve his performance. When Chaplin threatened Joshua Kimeto in this manner, Kimeto talked back to him, saying, "It doesn't matter. I could go back to Kenya and lead my normal life. So what if I was poor? It's better than feeling like a slave, being made to race all the time even when I'm injured."

Though Chaplin had little occasion to criticize my performance or threaten to deport me, he would exploit me not only by making me run multiple races in a single day (often times even when I had a slight injury or wasn't feeling well), but also by pitting me against the other Kenyans, asking them why they couldn't perform as well as I had or why they couldn't run three races in two days as I routinely did without complaining. In truth, I felt like complaining. I was just as disgruntled as the other Kenyans, but felt too intimidated at that point to talk back to Chaplin as they did.

Chaplin often mistook my timidity for subservience and used me as an intermediary between himself and other Kenyan runners. I remember one time in particular when Chaplin asked me to walk with him to the track while, in a very distraught tone, he complained about how Samson Kimombwa didn't want to run for him anymore. After convincing me to speak to Samson, Chaplin told me, "You are very good, Henry, and you are going to be the best. I know you worry about your education, but who cares?" This was typical of Chaplin's relationship with me. He would go from taking advantage of me or blatantly insulting me one minute to praising me the next.

Regardless of my uneasy relationship with Coach Chaplin, my first semester on the track was sparkling as I won one event after another leading up to my victory in the 1976 NCAA cross-country championships. During my WSU career, I would go on to win three NCAA cross-country championships, a feat only equaled by WSU alumnus Gerry Lindgren and the great University of Oregon runner

Steve Prefontaine. Unfortunately, my euphoria from winning my first cross-country championship was short-lived since, with the running season over, I no longer had the distraction of competition to take my mind off of my academic woes.

In December, as final exams approached, I became obsessed with the prospect of failing my classes. Coach Chaplin told me not to worry about classes since everything would take care of itself. He would try to comfort me by saying, "Hang in there, Henry, you'll get good grades." When I would respond by trying to tell him just how far behind I felt I was falling in my courses, he would interrupt me by saying, "Your feet will get you a degree. Don't worry."

Ultimately, Chaplin was dismissive of my educational needs. All he cared about was whether I passed my classes and remained eligible to compete. He cared nothing for my actual intellectual progress, which is what I cared about most. In fact, my intellectual success was much more important to me than my achievements on the track. I often felt abandoned by Chaplin, who seemed to have just set me free to sink or swim in the classroom. Perhaps Chaplin was in fact pulling strings without my knowing it, seeking favors from my professors to ensure that I would receive special treatment and remain eligible for the track season. Still, I didn't ask for these favors: I simply wanted to keep up with the other students and *earn*—as opposed to just being given—a passing grade. In the end, I ended up passing my classes and retaining my athletic eligibility my first semester, just as Coach Chaplin had predicted. However, the anxieties I experienced during this first semester—whether over my classroom inadequacies, my on-again, off-again relationship with Coach Chaplin, or his lack of genuine concern for my education—made me seek a new sanctuary where I could escape my worries—Cougar Cottage, where, after practice each afternoon, I would drink my fill until closing time.

Chapter VII
My Drinking Routine

At WSU, it wasn't that drinking interfered with my running routine so much as it became a part of it. Each day after my afternoon workout, I would head to the sauna to sweat out my body's toxins and fats. After I got out of the sauna, my muscles felt relaxed and rejuvenated, but my throat and mouth were parched by a thirst so deep that I felt only beer could quench it. At Cougar Cottage, I'd down pitcher after pitcher, quenching my thirst and washing my worries down with every glass until the bar closed at 2:00 AM, at which point I would stumble back to my apartment and, after finally gaining the appetite I suppressed through my long night of drinking, would scarf down some fast food before falling into a deep, drunken sleep for the few hours before Coach Chaplin would come to wake me up for my early morning run.

When I think back on the abuse I subjected my body to during my years at WSU, it is nothing short of a miracle that I was able to win the championships and break the records that I did. There were times when I won events still hung over from the previous night. On one occasion, in Berkeley in 1978, I even broke a world record with a hangover. Some people wonder how much greater my achievements would have been had I not been drinking heavily during this pinnacle of my running career. While my alcoholism certainly cut short my longevity as a runner, strangely, I don't believe it affected my best performances during my prime years at WSU. Of course, I would certainly prohibit any athlete from integrating heavy drinking into his or her training routine, and, in today's running world, where calorie counts and synthetic supplements have turned nutrition into a science, the idea of any serious runner also being a serious drinker seems absurd. Still, drinking was a self-defense mechanism for me, and it helped me alleviate the substantial stress I was experiencing both socially and in the classroom. Obviously, it was not a long-term solution for these anxieties, and, in fact, it only deferred my problems, making them more formidable when I finally did face up to them over a decade later. Still, learning to run with a temple-thumping hangover taught me something about discipline, about how to put mind over matter, and focus beyond my physical pain, no matter how excruciating. However absurd it may sound, heavy drinking was part of my routine during my years at WSU, and, though it would catch up to me later in life—resulting in terrible and far-reaching physical, social, and psychological consequences—I don't believe it slowed the times of my best or record-breaking performances at WSU.

Coach Chaplin was aware of my drinking from the first and, at times, even encouraging of it. In fact, he was much more worried about any romantic interests I had than he was about my drinking. For instance, when I started dating an American girl in 1977, my drinking subsided considerably. However, many of Coach Chaplin's comments to me at the time implied that he would rather me drink excessively than have me be preoccupied by a girlfriend. In regards to my success, Chaplin was ever the pragmatist. From my first semester at WSU, he knew that, despite heavy drinking, I was able to compete at a superior level; however, it soon became clear that once I was love struck, I was all but worthless on the track.

In many ways, my drinking habit alleviated whatever distrust I felt for Coach Chaplin. The more I drank, the more I started to block out and rebel against people around me who discouraged drinking. When I was drinking heavily, I even, at times, came to regard Chaplin as a good friend despite his unpredictability and frequently hostile behavior to me simply because he did not disapprove of my drinking. In fact, Chaplin would give me money in the evenings after every other workout, telling me, "Go have fun for a while before you go to bed."

Chapter VIII
The 1977 NCAA Indoor Championships

The night before the team was to leave for the 1977 NCAA Indoor Championships in Detroit, Samson Kimombwa and I got wasted. The next morning, as the rest of my teammates loaded luggage into the vehicles that would take us to the airport, I was in my room, still drunk and arguing with Coach Chaplin. I had gotten in so late the previous night that all I wanted to do was sleep a little more, so I told Chaplin to simply leave me the tickets and I would meet the team in Detroit. Of course, my request was unreasonable, and, after a few minutes of Chaplin's screaming at me to "get up, get dressed, and pack your bags, you son of a bitch," I finally submitted. As I look back on this confrontation, my obstinacy seems adolescent. However, at that time, as young and naïve as I was, it was the only way I knew how to rebel against Chaplin's controlling coaching tactics. Still, in beginning to rebel and push Chaplin's buttons, I was learning a few of his weaknesses. In many of his confrontations, he criticized my unpredictability and expressed his fear of my transferring to another college, and I soon realized that hinting that I might consider leaving WSU would weaken Chaplin's resolve.

In Detroit, I met Sammy Kipkurgat, a runner at the University of New Mexico (UNM), whom I knew from the Kenyan Army. We talked about how great it would be to go to the same university and especially a college where a number of my friends from the Kenyan Army went. Sammy said that his coach was interested in having me fly out to visit the UNM campus. Chaplin watched Sammy and me interact and was made visibly anxious by our conversation. Chaplin must have inferred what Sammy and I were talking about since, after he had wedged his way into our conversation, he expressed an interest in having Sammy visit Pullman.

Before the meet, the WSU squad was considered a favorite in the eyes of other schools' coaches. While Coach Chaplin arrived in Detroit with only one thing in mind—winning an NCAA championship—I had other motives. Doing well in the meets and helping my school win its first NCAA championship in any sport were certainly priorities; however, I was also interested in taking in the culture of a major American city with a vital Black American community, as well as in reconnecting with the many Kenyan runners attending various schools across the country. I, like many Kenyan runners, came to view NCAA championship meets as reunions in which I would have the chance to cut loose with fellow countrymen. These reunions were a way to help us forget the alienation most of us felt in our college communities, as well as the demeaning and exploitative tactics of many of our coaches.

In Detroit, Chaplin told me I was going to run the two-, three-, and one-mile races—all in two days. While the two- and three-mile races were distances I was accustomed to running, the mile was not my specialty or the focus of my training. To Chaplin, it came down to a simple equation: how can Rono earn the team the maximum number of points so as to bolster the team's standings? To win the championship, Chaplin decided he would have to ride me like the team's beast of burden, not caring how the heavy workload might wear down my body or compromise my ability to run at a peak level in each individual event.

I ran the two-mile with an NCAA record time and then won the three-mile with a course-best time. However, my exhaustion from these two victories made me hesitant about running an event that I had not prepared for. Still, Chaplin was insistent and came to me with despair in his voice, begging me to run the mile and saying, "Please, Henry, just do this for me. I know you are tired.

All you have to do is sit behind Steve Scott (who was a runner at UC-Irvine and the American record holder in the mile at the time), until halfway and then just sprint from there, and you will beat him. Wilson Waigwa will win the mile, but I'm begging you, just place in front of Steve Scott. That's all we need."

He looked into my eyes, and I looked away out of respect, but also out of shame since I noticed his eyes were tearing up and his voice was cracking as if he might break down. I had never seen Chaplin so emotional or vulnerable. Maybe it was simply an act or a ruse to make me run out of pity for him. Still, at that moment, his emotions seemed raw and real, and who's to say for sure that they weren't? Chaplin went on pleading, "Henry, all we need you to do is finish ahead of Scott, and we'll get the half point we need to win the NCAA Indoors."

As I prepared for the race, Chaplin was nervous, pacing around, and talking to himself. I followed Chaplin's strategy from the start, and, with two laps to go, I took the lead and began pulling away from the pack. The whole stadium rose, breathless, thinking that I, a middle-distance specialist, might be such a superior runner that I could even dominate an event I was not accustomed to running. However, my inexperience would catch up with me as Waigwa eventually overtook me, just as Chaplin had expected. I was nonetheless able to fend off Scott, who is still considered one of the best-ever U.S. milers, and, for this, Chaplin was ecstatic as my second-place finish earned our team the points we needed to edge out the University of Texas and claim the NCAA championship. It was the first NCAA championship WSU had claimed in any sport, and, the following day, sports headlines across the country had my name in them, touting my performance as the key to WSU's title.

Chapter IX
Heart Races

When our team returned to Pullman, we were greeted as heroes by a large, enthusiastic crowd that gathered in the stands of the coliseum to celebrate our victory. At that moment, however, I didn't feel like celebrating: I just wanted to be with my girlfriend, Liz. Chaplin told me to stick around so the team could be greeted, but I was tired of following his orders, and he knew he owed me a favor for running the mile. Now that I had relationship problems I needed to deal with, I needed some understanding. Chaplin let me meet my girlfriend and her parents in the office.

Liz sat behind me in my history class during my first semester, and soon she became my tutor and then my romantic interest. Though she and I dated steadily, I often felt uneasy about my relationship with her since she would often suddenly seem distant from me, especially when I had been away from her for the weekend at meets. Most of my teammates and Coach Chaplin warned me about dating an American girl, fearing that she might be using me for my fame or the money I promised to make once I turned pro.

Liz and her friends decided to throw a party to celebrate WSU's indoor championship. As we were driving to the party, one of Liz's friends pulled out a bottle of Wild Turkey and handed it to Mike Kosgei, who immediately chugged down half the bottle before passing it to me. I took it, closed my eyes, and, by the time I opened them, the bottle was empty. Kosgei started screaming, and I joined in with, "Kiptaragon, my village is great!"

I didn't have any food in my stomach, and, though I was accustomed to drinking more than my fair share of beer, I was not accustomed to drinking liquor. Mike and I were already plenty buzzed, and a long night of drinking lie ahead. Before the party, as Mike and I were waiting for the women to return from getting ready and freshening up, I complained to Kosgei about the mixed messages I had been receiving from Liz. Kosgei was two years ahead of me at WSU and had a much better understanding not only of English, but also of American women. He knew that I was naïve when it came to interacting with Americans, and he was always looking out for me, as if he were my older brother, to make sure people didn't take advantage of me. Kosgei had always expressed concern about Liz, and, though I didn't have any real evidence that Liz was using me, my complaints about her not wanting to sleep with me gave Kosgei the occasion to resume his tirade against American women in general and against Liz in particular. Kosgei told me, "Don't worry, Henry, I'll fix things. I'll do something about it." Later that evening, Kosgei asked Samson Kimombwa what he thought about Liz, and Samson agreed that she wasn't the right girl for me and that she probably had ulterior motives for dating me.

I didn't understand where I stood with Liz, and my frustration about my relationship with her only aggravated my feelings of alienation in general. I wasn't an American. I was a Kenyan, and, though I didn't understand how to interact with American girls or act in a socially acceptable manner, I knew that the core of my character was sound. In Kenya, I was a person whose character could be easily perceived and appreciated, but, in America, the virtues that would be apparent within my native culture were often mocked and chastised. I had African kindness, which, to American women, implied weakness and impotence. Whenever I thought about this, it just made me want to drink even more.

At the party, Kosgei continued to confront me about my relationship with Liz. I would later realize that Kosgei didn't have a problem with Liz personally, but that he simply felt we were incompatible and, since he believed there would be no hope of our having a lasting, meaningful relationship, he considered her a distraction from me reaching my potential as a runner. Kosgei would remind me that most college girls like Liz are from affluent families in the richest country in the world while I was from a tribal background in the Third World.

After we had been at the party for a while, still drinking, Kosgei began speaking openly in front of Liz and her friends about his suspicions regarding Liz's relationship with me. He said that Liz only wanted to take advantage of me and demanded to know what she wanted from me. One of Liz's friends stood up for her and began calling Kosgei names. Kosgei became flustered because he wanted to open up a dialogue with Liz and her friends so as to be clear that he would not stand for her manipulating me in any way. Liz's friend cursed Mike more loudly until Mike became so outraged that he screamed at the top of his lungs and then turned over the table we were sitting at. Beer bottles flew from the table, some hitting the ceiling and shattering everywhere. I moved to protect Liz, standing between her and Kosgei. Everyone around the table was sprayed with beer, which continued to drip from the ceiling as the house went silent, with everyone trying to figure out what had just transpired. Kosgei left the party with his roommate, taking off his shirt as he walked home, still visibly angry—so angry, in fact, that halfway home, he laid himself down on the side of the road in an attempt to get a hold of his emotions.

The following morning, Liz's mother called Mike, and I listened to the conversation on the other line. I knew that Kosgei had acted inappropriately, but I also appreciated his concern for me. Kosgei simply wanted people to be upfront and honest with me because I was inexperienced and vulnerable. Over the phone, Mike explained to Liz's mother his reasons for questioning Liz's intentions, as well as his reasons for being so protective of me. While he expressed remorse for the outburst, he also explained that it came from his frustration at not being able to bridge the cultural misunderstandings between him and Liz. He said his violent actions had resulted from his inability to civilly explain, as well as Liz's friends' inability to listen to, his reasons for doubting Liz. Liz's mother was both patient and sympathetic toward Mike, and it was clear that she sympathized with how cultural misunderstandings had made the situation at the party become volatile. Liz's mother insisted that Mike go to the police station to write a statement of what happened at the party. I accompanied Mike to serve as a witness for him; however, when I was writing my statement, I found it difficult to communicate what had happened at the party, not only because it was still difficult for me to write in English, but also because I didn't want to implicate Mike in a crime. After comparing my statement to Mike's, the policeman realized my statement was, if not biased, then at least very selective in its details, and he did not pressure me to give additional statements.

On the phone, Liz's mother told Kosgei that she would like Liz and him to exchange gifts to show that there were no hard feelings. Mike did not bring a gift for Liz since to do so, he said, would be to admit that he was at fault. Still, he graciously accepted Liz's gift, which was a cake she had baked, and said, pointing to his stomach with a big grin on his face, it will go straight here. Everyone laughed, and it seemed that the whole incident had been resolved as best it could be.

Despite all this, however, my relationships problems with Liz remained unresolved. After the incident, she stopped returning my phone calls. In retrospect, I was acting maniacally, doing things that would have been entirely inappropriate to an American college girl like calling her as late as 2:00 AM. Out of my loneliness, confusion, and frustration, I began binge drinking, which only made me more manic, sinking me deeper in despair.

When the outdoor track meets were about to get started in the early spring of 1977, Chaplin arranged a team meeting. I was too heartbroken to attend and told my teammates to tell Chaplin I was going to sit out the upcoming meet in Idaho and stay in Pullman. Later that day, Chaplin called me, trying to get me to change my mind and come to Idaho. Chaplin said that people in Pullman loved me. I thought to myself, if that's true, why won't my girlfriend return my calls?

Not long after I got off the phone with Chaplin, Liz called and asked me to go for a run with her. I figured coach probably called her and was trying to use her as a means to get me to go to Idaho. But I was so desperate to see Liz that I didn't care, and so I accepted her invitation. While we were jogging, she told me that she now realized that Africans, when they first arrive in America, are too shy to say what they mean. I agreed and, after cooling down from our run, we went to drink some tea. Afterward, she asked me if I planned to rejoin the team, but I was hesitant to reply. While I was happy to see Liz, I also felt as though she and I were both being manipulated by Chaplin and that this encounter was merely his ploy to get me to go to Idaho.

After we finished our tea, she told me she had to go home and that, on my way back to my room, I should be sure to look both ways before crossing the street as I had a reputation on campus for walking around staring straight forward without turning my head even when walking in the street. I went home, depressed but not as manic, and, after a while, I fell into a deep, hard sleep. The following morning, Chaplin's wife picked me up to take me to the meet in Idaho. I was still upset and didn't want to go, but I left for

Idaho anyway. When we arrived in Idaho, Chaplin gave me $50 as if money—or the six packs that the quick cash would afford Samson and me—could solve my problems.

Chapter X
Pressures From Chaplin

Though I suspected that Coach Chaplin used Liz to get me to compete in the Idaho meet, it was still apparent that he disapproved of my relationship with her. In fact, Chaplin's critique of my relationship with Liz was about the only thing that he and Mike Kosgei saw eye-to-eye on. During the Idaho meet, Kosgei became more openly critical of Chaplin's handling of Kenyan athletes and especially critical of his handling of me. He told Chaplin, gesturing to me, "You brought this Kenyan who grew up in poverty with almost no education to an American university and expect him to survive in college?"

Kosgei and his roommate, fellow Kenyan Jonathon Nge'no, came from much stronger educational backgrounds than my own and were critical of the university's athletic department for recruiting athletes who were not prepared for the rigors of university academics or the culture shock of interacting in a predominantly White college town. However, they both also appreciated the plight of poor Kenyans such as me and how few opportunities there were for them to escape from a life of poverty to one of education and prosperity. As a result, Kosgei and Nge'no didn't blame me for taking advantage of the opportunity offered to me or even of the recruitment of athletes such as myself; instead, they were critical of the way in which an athletic department took so little interest in fostering an environment conducive to the education of its athletes. Kosgei and Nge'no were upset because Coach Chaplin would rather try to persuade instructors to "go easy" on their athletes than to provide the academic assistance such as tutors and translators that would allow athletes to actually become engaged by their school work.

Chaplin began to fear that Kosgei's comments might make me rebel, and soon Chaplin began criticizing Kosgei during our private conversations. Chaplin told me that whenever I have a problem, I should seek help from him, not Kosgei, who he said was misleading me.

Eventually, Chaplin threatened to cut Kosgei from the team. Kosgei was a perceptive person, and he realized that I was a faithful friend to him and that Chaplin would not dare to do anything that might influence me to transfer to another school. Kosgei had me call Chaplin and ask him why he was threatening to kick him out of the program. Chaplin said he was tired of Kosgei's making every issue involving our team political and that he could no longer tolerate Kosgei's poor running performance. I only had to say one sentence to get Chaplin to change his tune: "If Kosgei goes, I go with him." After that, Chaplin's assaults on Kosgei ended, and Kosgei came to realize how easily he could use me to manipulate Chaplin. For instance, Nge'no, who was very scholarly and would later become a professor of economics, needed two things that Chaplin could help him with: a PE credit in order to graduate and a part-time job. Though Chaplin could have easily found Nge'no a position working in the school gymnasium, he simply couldn't bring himself to help any African who wasn't running for him. Dr. Nge'no was a dedicated scholar who never left his books out of his sight, and he consistently received A-grades. However, he received a D in Coach Chaplin's PE course, and he and Kosgei felt this was Chaplin's way of getting back at them for using me to manipulate him.

While Coach Chaplin's interests in me were largely selfish, he often served as my only advocate against a swell of hostile pundits and journalists—both American and Kenyan—who ridiculed my poor college credentials. Isaiah Kiplagat, the secretary general of the KAAA at the time, was the most outspoken of these critics. In a

Kenyan newspaper in 1977, Kiplagat blamed American universities for admitting foreign runners "like Henry Rono, whose standard of education is elementary." Soon, many public officials were calling for athletes who had defected from the Kenyan Army or the KAAA to be deported back to Kenya. The prospect of being deported frightened me, and the criticism about my education struck a personal nerve. Though I didn't have a strong primary education, I was intent upon improving my education through college and not simply letting my feet earn my diploma. When a reporter from the student newspaper asked me for an interview about my college credentials, I told him to first okay the interview with Coach Chaplin. The following day, the interview was set up in Chaplin's office. While Chaplin let me speak freely, he also clarified my statements, telling the reporter that I was not in college simply to learn how to run or otherwise I would have stayed in Kenya like my hero, Kip Keino. Chaplain maintained that I came to college to get an education that would prepare me for a career beyond running, and I was using my running talent to pay for my college tuition. Probably Chaplin was simply saying what was politically correct, but, in this case, his words echoed my very sentiment.

By the summer of 1977, Chaplin went from being my newfound public spokesperson and advocate to becoming my greatest source of stress through his boisterous public rants about my "unbounded running potential." Chaplin's public comments about me were so full of praise and expectation that I began to internalize the burden to perform at a level never before achieved by a middle-distance runner. After watching me finish ahead of the American record holder in the mile at the NCAA championships in Detroit and then hearing of my victory in a half-marathon in Puerto Rico, Chaplin boasted that "Henry Rono will break every world record from one mile to the marathon." Of course, such predictions were outlandish to say the least, and they only added to the other anxieties I felt from my hardships in the classroom to my social awkwardness, my turbulent love life, and my tensions with the KAAA. All of these pressures and anxieties made me more reliant on alcohol as a means to calm my nerves. I stopped eating, but kept binge drinking to help me sleep.

Chapter XI
A Mysterious Illness

By the late fall of 1977, my anxiety and my alcoholism combined to wear down my body and nerves. I began to notice dark blood in my stool. The doctors told me I had bleeding ulcers and that, if I didn't take better care of myself, I could eventually die from the condition. During races, my legs were dragging, and, by the 1977 NCAA Outdoor Championships in Champaign, Illinois, I lost my self-confidence. In Champaign, I only placed second in the 3,000-meter steeplechase even though, on account of my condition, Chaplin refrained from doubling me up in events as he was accustomed to doing. Even though I was ill, every time I stepped to the starting line, my opponents were still intimidated by me, which made them run tensely and allowed me to still place in most races even though I was a far cry from my peak running condition.

After the Champaign meet, Coach Chaplin began to realize the immense amount of stress I was under and asked me if I would be returning to WSU in the fall. I told him I didn't know. After the NCAA Championship, I was invited to compete in Germany along with Samson Kimombwa on a trip sponsored by Adidas and arranged by Gordon Cooper, who was acting as my agent. In Germany, I became more ill. Though the Finnish reporter, Pekka Rinne, celebrated my competing in Europe and hailed the possibility of my breaking records in Germany, my sickness forced me to fly back to the United States to seek additional medical attention.

Cooper arranged for me to see a specialist in California, who examined me from head to toe and took blood samples repeatedly without ever discovering what was causing my illness. I became frustrated with the doctors, telling them, "You guys are stupid. You keep taking my blood all the time yet you can't find what is wrong with me. Taking blood from me one or two times is fine, but why all the time?" While I was undergoing tests at the doctor's office one morning, I saw on the front page of the sports section that my friend Samson Kimombwa had broken the 10,000-meter record by half a second, running it in 27:30.

Hearing about the record made me impatient with my illness and especially impatient with the inconclusive tests and ineffective treatment I was receiving. I started putting pressure on Gordon Cooper to find events in which I could run and break Kimombwa's new record. I told him I wanted to go to the All-African Games, to which he replied, "Wait, you haven't recovered yet." During my illness, I was working on Cooper's farm, pulling up weeds and thinking about world records. All the while, in papers across Europe, Pekka Rinne was once again touting my record-breaking potential in a variety of events, writing, "Henry Rono would break all middle-distance world records from 3,000 to 10,000 meters if he were here in Europe." I began to think that maybe he was right. The best antidote to my illness seemed to be my growing excitement at the opportunity to compete for world records.

Chapter XII
The First of Many Comebacks

Cooper bought me a ticket to the All-African Games in Tunis. I flew via London, where I got stranded for a few days. I met the chairman of the KAAA, Samson Ongeri, at Heathrow Airport, and he assured me that everything was in place to assure an easy trip to Tunis. However, in London, I had troubles with my connection and was stuck there for a great while. When I finally arrived in Tunis, I was stranded in the airport there even longer than I had been in London as no one came to pick me up. I trusted that Ongeri would take care of my trip, arranging for smooth connections and a ride from the airport. After all, I always heard him warning about Western agencies, managers, and agents who would take advantage of naïve African runners, using poor Kenyan athletes to make themselves a fortune. His words began to ring hollow as I waited and waited at the airport, unsure of what to do or where to go. It was becoming ever clearer to me that if the American agencies and agents were corrupt, they were no more so than the Kenyan officials—at least they are professional, never leaving you to fend for yourself in a foreign airport!

When I finally arrived at the hotel where the Kenyan team was staying, it was late at night, and all my friends on the team were already sleeping. In the morning, everyone on the team was excited to see me, and they were asking me a lot of questions about the United States and why I was sick. All I could tell them was that the doctors were taking a lot of blood out of me without ever finding the cause of my illness.

The All-African Games went very well for me. I was still recovering from my illness, so my body would not allow me to dominate races as I hoped I would; still, I was able to prove that, even in less than optimal shape, I could hold my own against the best runners in the world. I placed third in 5,000-meters and second in the 3,000-steeplechase. After the All-African Games, I went to Europe for a few meets. In Italy, I won the 5,000-meters and ran into my old Olympic coach and hero, Kip Keino, who told me, "You will soon break the world record for the 5,000 meters in 13:07."

Olympic Dream

I attended that year's International Association of Athletic Federations (IAAF) World Cup in Düsseldorf, Germany, but did not enter any races there. Instead, I watched the events and was inspired by the performance of the Ethiopian runner, Maruss Hiffter, who won both the 5,000- and 10,000-meter races. Seeing or hearing about other runners like Hiffter or my friend, Samson Kimombwa, performing at their peaks gave me the strength to train harder. After the IAAF competitions, I competed in a few meets before the end of the European season, running in London and in a couple of meets in Germany before heading back to WSU with my confidence restored and my head back on straight.

After traveling throughout Europe during the summer, I felt more mature and able to adjust to the cultural and social challenges of college life in Pullman. I also began to be more assertive in my interactions with Coach Chaplin, telling him to be more conscientious of my body and not double me up in so many events—practices that I believed contributed to my ulcer. That fall, I went the entire cross-country season unchallenged before claiming my second NCAA cross-country championship.

In January 1978, I ran an indoor in San Diego before flying to Auckland, New Zealand for a 10,000-meters world-record attempt in which I fell well short with a time of 27:47. Still, runners there were impressed by my performance, and José Hermann told me he thought I was capable of breaking world records in the upcoming season. I flew directly from New Zealand to Puerto Rico for the half-marathon, which I won in 64 minutes.

When workouts began in the spring of 1978, I told Coach Chaplin I planned my own training regimen and would simply need him to follow my formula, hold the stopwatch, call out split times, and not make too much noise. On Tuesday of week one of my training, I ran 400 meters times 12 with one-minute intervals. On that Thursday, I ran six 800-meters with one-minute intervals. During week two, I ran five 1,000-meters with one-minute intervals and two 100-meters 24 times with 30-second intervals. This routine allowed me to prepare myself to run for a variety of race lengths from the low middle-distances to the marathon. During this training, I kept my morning run at its usual six to eight miles, which is the same distance I had run ever since I was in Gilgil.

In that year's NCAA Indoor Championship, I ran two and three miles unchallenged. However, with the mile, my performance was less impressive as I ran the slowest mile of anyone in the field. My poor performance in the mile could be attributed to a number of factors from fatigue after dominating the other two races I ran in the meet to not having emphasized distances under two miles in my training. Still, I was satisfied with my overall performance at the Indoor Championships and told Coach Chaplin that I was ready to break four world records the upcoming spring outdoor season and, specifically, that I had my sights on the 3,000 meters, the 3,000-steeplechase, the 5,000 meters, and the 10,000 meters.

Early in the spring season, I tuned up my running in San Jose, California, running the 3,000 meters in 7:57. After that meet, Coach Chaplin said that Jeff Hollister from Nike wanted to talk to me about my future running plans. Hollister told me that they expected great things from me and were wondering if I would consider signing an exclusive contract to wear their apparel when I graduated. I told them yes, so long as Nike treated me fairly and paid me more than other companies, I would have no problem promoting their product. After meeting with the representatives from Nike, I flew back to Pullman, Washington, where many of my friends and teammates were impressed that Nike was pursuing me. However, I was not impressed by Nike's interest in me as I had more important things on my mind, namely preparing for the world records I intended to break. During the meets early in the outdoor season, I felt myself progressively returning to the peak form I had before my long illness and then surpassing that form, reaching a new pinnacle in my running. To me, anything seemed possible.

Chapter XIII
Eighty Days of Joy

In the early spring of 1978, I had it all planned out: I would begin my assault on a series of four middle-distance world records by first setting my sights on improving my time in the 5,000 meters. My first 5,000-meter race of that spring was in San Jose, California, where I ran a 13:32. In another meet two weeks later, I ran a 13:22 and felt my progress could allow me to set the world record in my next 5,000-meter race. This race happened to be in Berkeley, California on April 8, where—despite the fact that I had drank with great abandon with friends the night before and spent most of that morning trying to shake a hangover—I ran a 13:08.4, which knocked 4.5 seconds off of Dick Quix's world record. After the race, Mike Kosgei told me, "I will be telling my folks in Kenya that I have not seen anything like this." I had never experienced such exhilaration after any victory, and the beautiful thing about that day is that Kosgei, as well as many of my teammates, seemed just as excited about my performance as I was.

The next record I put in my sights was the 3,000-meter steeplechase. On May 6, I was running at a record clip in a beautiful track venue at the University of Oregon and in front of what are perhaps the most enthusiastic track-and-field fans in the United States. The Oregon fans—having witnessed the incredible accomplishments of the late Steve Prefontaine only a few years previously—knew greatness when they saw it, and, halfway through the race, as it became apparent that I stood not only to break the world-record time but to shatter it, the crowd stood up in anticipation and cheered me, a member of their rival team, on toward the finish line.

Suddenly, out of nowhere, Coach Chaplin jumped out onto the track, waving a white towel. At first, I thought he was rooting me on, and, only seconds later, did I realize he wanted me to stop.

"This state doesn't deserve the world record," Chaplin said.

Stunned, I walked off the track crestfallen. Confused, I watched Chaplin and Oregon coach Bill Dillenger yell at one another as members of the press swarmed me. "Get away from him," Chaplin yelled at the journalists. The jeers at Haywood Field became louder and louder as many disgruntled fans poured onto the field to confront Chaplin personally. Later, when things had settled down and we had been escorted safely from the field, Chaplin told me, "I didn't want you to give them the privilege at their meet. Oregon's program doesn't appreciate or recruit African runners. They're bigots and they don't appreciate me or my program in the first place." Realizing how upset I was, Chaplin then tried to reassure me, saying, "It's not you, Henry. They just don't like me at all."

This event came to symbolize a great deal to me about the contradictions in Coach Chaplin's character. Though it's true that WSU recruited more African runners than Oregon, I always thought this had less to do with Coach Chaplin being socially progressive and more to do with his being opportunistic. Chaplin's comments that day at Haywood Field at least insinuated that he considered himself to be a progressive-minded, socially enlightened individual; however, if he were such an advocate for African runners, then why wouldn't he let me claim the record I had worked so hard for? Even if it were true that the Oregon running program or the fans at Haywood Field that day were bigots—which, at least in regard to their enthusiastic applause as I closed in on the record, they seemed not to be—was Chaplin's spite so great, his jealousy and hatred of Coach Dillenger's program so deep, that he would ignore my hopes of breaking the record I most certainly would have shattered that day? Though Chaplin may have claimed to stop me in order to take a stand against the bigotry of the Oregon program or fans, in truth, he acted bigotedly by treating me as a thing—a piece of property he could tell when to stop and when to go with no consideration for my feelings and aspirations. However, paradoxically, his stopping me also proved what great respect he had for my strength of mind and the confidence he had in my running ability as he had absolutely no doubt that I would go on to break the record in my next attempt at it.

That next attempt would come the following week in Seahawks' Stadium in Seattle, Washington. The evening before the meet, Mike Kosgei had invited me and a number of his friends out to dinner to commemorate my attempt at the 3,000-meter steeplechase record the following day. He asked me for a prediction of my time in tomorrow's race, and I jotted 8:04 on a napkin. Though the running conditions on that cool, rainy day in Seattle were less than optimal, I nonetheless finished the race in 8:05.4, shaving 2.6 seconds off Swede Anders Garderud's record. After this race, my emotions were more restrained than they had been after my record-breaking performance in Berkeley a few weeks earlier, and Kosgei asked, "How come you seem like you haven't accomplished anything? You're not even smiling." I looked down and shook my head. "Not yet," I told him, "I still have two to go."

My attempt to claim the world record in the 10,000 meters would have to wait until the European season. Mike Boit put me in contact with a meet director from Germany who signed me up for a 10,000-meter race in Vienna, Austria. In Vienna, as I was ducking into the taxi that would take me from the airport, the Austrian press surrounded the vehicle, and one journalist blurted out, "What time will you be putting down tomorrow in the 10K?" As I closed the door behind me, I responded without any hesitation, "27:22."

It was June 11, and the entire field for the 10,000 meters got off to a sluggish start. Still, I was leading and, with half of the 10,000 meters behind me, I heard the announcer say that I was four seconds off world-record pace. Though I was well off the pace I intended for the race, I realized that I was nonetheless still within striking distance of the record. I ran the last 5,000 meters in high gear, bringing the last of the 25 laps home in 56 seconds to finish the race in 27:22, cutting eight seconds off the record set the previous summer by my friend and countryman, Samson Kimombwa. When I saw the meet director after the race, he was overcome with tears of joy, elated that I had not only delivered the world record I had promised him, but that I had done it in the exact time I had predicted the previous day.

I would make my attempt at the 3,000-meter record in Oslo, Norway, which was a fortunate coincidence for me as I would have the opportunity to complete the most prolific assault on the record books by any distance runner in front of some of the world's most enthusiastic and knowledgeable track-and-field fans. My roommate, Mike Boit, and I woke up early that morning for our warm up, running through the lush, mountainous Norwegian forest. After our muscles were good and loose, Boit said, "It looks like we've done enough warming up." I told him that I wanted to run up a particularly steep hill a few times. "For how long?" Boit asked, looking at me with a tilted head and exasperated expression. I told him 45 minutes would steam us up nice and good. "Aren't you going for the world record today?" he asked. "Yes," I responded, "But not until after I've had my share of this hill." When I was done with the hill and we were heading back to the hotel, Boit kept questioning me about why I wanted to have such an exhausting warm up when I intended to challenge the world record later that day. "Just wait and see," I responded, "I'll take the world record today by 3, maybe 5, seconds."

That evening of June 27, when the announcer introduced me to the crowd of 30,000 spectators, the whole stadium went silent. The intense anticipation of the large crowd was obvious, and they remained relatively quiet as I began the race at an easy clip, moving at a pace as natural for me as the flow of water was to the stream that Mike and I ran alongside on our morning warm up through the forest. The front-runners completed the first mile in 4:04, which was a slower pace than I had hoped for. Still, I thought perhaps the world record might be attainable. I shot from the back of the pack like a rocket, and the crowd stood up, wondering if maybe I could overcome my slow start to make track-and-field history. I streaked 50 meters ahead of every runner and held this surge of speed for the final three-and-a-half laps, completing the race in 7:32.1, which improved upon Brendan Foster's record by 3.1 seconds. When it was announced over the PA system that I had indeed set a new world record, the whole stadium came alive all at once with a voice as resounding as thunder. I took two victory laps around the stadium, shaking hands with everyone I could. I had accomplished my most ambitious athletic goal, which had seemed only a vague pipedream just a summer earlier, when I was recovering from emotional distress and battling an intense and mysterious physical ailment.

Repeatedly since that victory in Oslo, journalists, fans, coaches, and other athletes have asked how I was able to accomplish such an implausible feat, breaking four middle-distance records in such a short span of time. Others wondered why I and not another more established or well-known runner such as Gabre Sellasie, who had perhaps shown greater potential than I in the months leading up to the spring of 1978, achieved these unprecedented accomplishments. I could simply tell them that when you have the right formula, you get the right answer. Unlike the great Moroccan and Ethiopian runners who set up their equations with two unknown variables, relying on rabbits to set their pace, my formula has always been to trust my keen sense of self-awareness, which allows me to set my pace based upon my understanding of the potential of my mind and body to perform on a given day.

Chapter XIV
Fallout

While my historic record-breaking streak brought me more joy than any of my accomplishments in track and field, paradoxically, it also became the greatest obstacle to my pursuit of an independent running career. To meet organizers, I was no longer just a great runner they desired to have in their events: I became a commodity they had to get by any means necessary. To Kenyan athletic officials, my career was no longer one they wished to manipulate: it became the one athletic career they felt it necessary to either control or destroy. For members of the Kenyan national team, I was no longer a teammate and peer: I became the person upon whom their being able to race and make money in foreign meets depended. To Coach John Chaplin, I was no longer just his star pupil: I became a pocket full of corporate sponsorships that he wished to get his hands into.

Still, my records brought me joy worth the cost of the bureaucratic greed that was thrust upon me. While the officials, coaches, and politicians who attempted to exploit and manipulate me following my successes in 1978 may have been able to deter my career and take my money away, they will never be able to take away the accolades I received from track-and-field fans and historians following my record-breaking streak. Few things could make me prouder than the claim of some sportswriters that, in the year of 1978, I was not only the greatest runner in the world, but the greatest athlete period. Few things could make me happier than the memory of hearing my name alongside those of Viren, Zatopek, and Nurmi, the greatest distance runners of all time.

Conflict began almost immediately for me after achieving the fourth of my world records. There was great pride in Kenya for my records, and I felt not only a responsibility, but a great desire to share my accomplishments with my countrymen. Though I wasn't entirely ready to reconcile with the KAAA, I wanted to return to Kenya to greet my fans and family. There were also requests from President Jomo Kenyatta to honor me as a national hero.

If I returned to Kenya, I realized I would have to resume a functional and at least halfway cordial relationship with the KAAA.

The KAAA understood my desire to return to Kenya and to compete with the national team, and, though they also knew I was a runner who valued independence and autonomy over my athletic career, beginning in the summer of 1978, they would make every attempt to tie up my career and make me submit to their every wish. I had learned my lesson, not only from my short experience competing under KAAA rule before defecting from the Kenyan Army to attend WSU, but also from watching how the organization had sucked dry other elite runners such as Kip Keino, who, despite all of his records, was still living at the mercy of the KAAA and provided only with a humble coaching salary. From the first, KAAA officials realized that I was a runner so focused on my craft that I would not be easily persuaded through monetary bribes. As a result, the KAAA understood that if they wished to persuade Henry Rono to compete in an event with the Kenyan national team, they would have to use his friends and countrymen as pawns to try and manipulate him.

Soon after my victory in Oslo, Mike Boit told me of a threatening letter he received from the KAAA, which listed a series of meets they demanded I take part in. Their demands were complicated by the fact that the Kenyan team's entry into many of these events, according to the meet directors, was contingent upon my participation. If I decided not to compete, many of my friends on the Kenyan team would be unable to participate in these events and so would lose out on much-needed paychecks from these meets. After my exhausting 81 days of record breaking, I was both emotionally and physically exhausted, and I wanted nothing more than to take a good, long rest during which time I would be able to meditate on what my running future would hold—whether I would return to WSU for my senior year or turn professional. Still, I felt obligated to attend the first meet in which the KAAA so forcefully requested my participation. I headed to the meet in Italy and, despite the fact I had nothing left in my joints, ran well enough to win the 5,000 meters.

After the race, there was a great deal of tension between KAAA general secretary Robert Ouko and Mike Boit. The word was that the meet director and Ouko both felt they had been shortchanged, and Ouko blamed this discrepancy in payoffs on Boit, who had served as the intermediary between me, the KAAA, and the Italian meet director. Ouko called for a meeting between him and the Kenyan team, in which he tried to reassure us that he was not trying to swindle anyone: not Mike Boit, not Henry Rono, and certainly not the Italian meet director. "I don't want Henry Rono to have a bad impression of me," Ouko said, "I simply don't want to be fired from my job. I just want to have my share." As if to provide me a gesture of his goodwill, he then announced that I had been selected as Kenya's flag carrier for the All-African Games and the Commonwealth Games. After Ouko finished speaking to the team, the Italian meet director also called his own meeting with the Kenyan team. He said he noticed two factions forming among the Kenyan athletes, and he expressed his wish for us to retain team solidarity.

At the time, perhaps I did not fully realize that the factions the Italian meet director spoke of were drawn around me. Many of my teammates, such as Mike Boit, whether just jealous or simply pragmatic, thought it was unfair that their own running prospects and paychecks were dependent on whether I decided to compete with the team for a given meet. These teammates thought they should be allowed to travel and compete in the meets that I refused to attend. Other teammates realized that I was the key that unlocked opportunities for them to compete in meets they otherwise would not be invited to. Neither of these factions was hostile to me; each realized that I wasn't a troublemaker and that I was supportive of my teammates' careers. Most of them also sympathized with my situation, realizing that the demands put upon me by the KAAA were unreasonable and could take a severe toll on my running career, as well as theirs.

After the Italian meet, the team flew back to Kenya and headed to training camp in Nyeri. From Nyeri, we left for the state house in Mombassa, where our team was to be received by President Kenyatta and I was to be presented with the flag to carry to the All-

African and Commonwealth Games. While Kenyatta was growing old and senile at times, his speech to us that day was eloquent. He told us, "I know politics, not sports; however, whether you are an athlete or politician, you must treat others the way you want to be treated; also, you must treat yourself as you want to be treated." As a sign of how hungry the coaches and athletes were for fair compensation for their hard work and talents, throughout the ceremony, Mike Boit kept asking me if Ongeri was going to give me anything, and, after I received the flag, Kip Keino only wanted to know whether Kenyatta had also given me a monetary reward.

After the ceremony, the team left for Algeria, where I won two gold medals in the All-African Games. After the All-African Games, we headed to Edmonton, in Alberta, Canada, for the Commonwealth Games, where I again claimed two gold medals. After the competition, the team was to head back to Kenya. It had been a long and prosperous season for me as I returned home with four world records and four gold medals. I was exhausted and in sore need of a break, though the KAAA and European meet directors thought otherwise. To them, I was merely a commodity.

A great deal of pressure was put on me by my teammates in the athletes' village at the Commonwealth Games as Mike Boit had been in contact with a meet director in Zurich who said he and other members of the team could compete in the event so long as Henry

Rono would participate. Though he knew I was exhausted, Boit started putting pressure on me. He wanted me to abandon my responsibility to return the national flag to Kenyatta and take off with him and the other member of the team to Zurich. Boit told me to simply hand over the flag to boxer Stephen Muchoki. I began to suspect that it was not merely greed that was motivating Boit, but probably a tinge of jealousy as well. At the 1976 Olympics, he wanted to be a team captain and flag carrier, but ended up losing out to Charles Asati.

For once, even the KAAA was on my side, saying the entire team should return home and fulfill our responsibility to return the flag to Kenyatta. However, Boit continued to pressure me to buck the KAAA's authority. Before I realized what was happening, Boit was taking a vote, asking which runners wanted to return home with the officials and Henry Rono and which athletes wanted to head to Zurich to compete. At first, I thought he was simply posturing since the Zurich meet director had made it clear that none of the other members of the Kenyan team would be allowed to race without me. Still, Boit had his share of influential advocates, including Kip Keino, who tried to convince me to go, saying, "Look at me. I ran for the Kenyan flag and what was I given in return? What do you think, that they'll treat you differently?" In a bold move, Boit hastily gathered the assenting athletes and left for the airport to catch a flight for Zurich.

Unfortunately for Boit, he and his renegade group of runners were stranded mid-route at Heathrow Airport in London until the Zurich meet director was fooled into believing that I was with them, at which point he promptly provided tickets for the group. When they arrived in London's Heathrow Airport, all the meet director wanted to know was, "Where is Henry Rono?" He told Boit the meet could not go on without me. As a result, Boit and his group kept putting pressure not only on me, but also on the KAAA officials, who were still in the athletes' village in Edmonton, to convince them that it was in their best interest to have me compete in Zurich. Eventually, Ongeri caved in and instructed Mike Sang—who was one of the few KAAA officials who wasn't corrupt and who took the athletes' best interests to heart—to meet up with Boit and his renegades at Heathrow Airport. Apprehensive and upset, I hastily bundled up the Kenyan flag and gathered my luggage. "Don't lose the flag," Sang told me, "You need to take it back to the person who gave it to you."

As soon as I arrived in Zurich, the meet director, Andrea Broker, called a meeting for Boit, Sang, and me. The bickering between the three of them went on until I told them I came here to run and not for issues of personal greed or politics. Sang came out of that meeting no longer trusting Boit. He emphasized that Boit and Andrea knew each other well and communicated in secret and that they were not only trying to manipulate me, but also other Kenyan athletes and even officials. I ran in that meet unchallenged, surprised that my legs still had any spring in them at all after such a long, hard season.

After the meet, Mike Sang told me, "We'd better hurry to the airport. You need to get the flag to President Kenyatta as soon as possible." Kenyatta had been ill, and Sang was afraid that he might pass away before we were able to return the flag to him. We traveled from the airport to Nairobi's civic center, where a large crowd was rallying in the street and becoming impatient to see me, saying that if they didn't see Rono soon, stones would fly. The KAAA Chairman, Isaiah Kiplagat, couldn't calm the crowd down, so they rushed the police to the Serena Hotel to escort me to the rally as quickly as possible. When we arrived at the rally, members of the crowd picked me up and raised me above their heads for all the people to see me. It was one of the most exhilarating and surreal moments of my life.

The morning after the rally, I was rushed back to the airport to catch a flight to Mombassa, where the members of the Kenyan team who remained at the Commonwealth games were to attend a ceremony hosted by President Kenyatta at the statehouse. It was August 20, 1978, and, although it would end up being the last public ceremony attended by President Kenyatta, Kenyatta looked like he might live for another 10 years as he addressed the attendees personally and with a great amount of eloquence and tact. After

I handed over the flag to him, he honored me with The Order of the Burning Spear, second class—which is the second highest honor that the President can bestow upon a Kenyan citizen. At the ceremony, Kenyatta also honored boxer Stephen Muchoki as Elder of the Burning Spear (EBS) third class.

Before he gave us his final speech, Kenyatta pulled a long sword from its sheath and raised it above his head to shimmer in the room's bright lights. Then he told us, "Your success has made you free. You can go anywhere in this world, and people will respect you as a Kenyan. You will be feared for your talents." After the ceremony, the Minister of State, Mbiu Koinange, called me aside and, pointing to the gathering of people, said, "You see these people? You are a very important person to them." They served supper, and I was seated close to President Kenyatta and his wife, Mama Ngina.

The following day, I was supposed to fly to London to run with the English runner and soon-to-be Olympic gold medallist Steve Ovett. I began to notice that all the radios were playing the Kenyan national anthem repeatedly. In the streets of Nairobi, people were silent, walking around with their heads down and not interacting, which added to the eeriness of that cloudy day. Finally, I received word that President Kenyatta had died, and, out of respect for him, I cancelled my trip to compete in London.

So began the second presidential era of post-colonial Kenya as Kenyatta's Vice President, Daniel arap Moi, assumed leadership of the country. This regime change had terrible and far-reaching effects on Nandis, many of whom feared and opposed Moi's transition into power. Soon, Moi's government started interrogating even 10-year-old kids about their parents' political affiliations. Such techniques foreshadowed more brutal practices to follow as Moi's regime would not only threaten his political opponents, but often have them killed in the most terrible and archaic ways. Soon, many Nandi elders would say that they felt as though oppressive colonial rule had returned.

About a year after Kenyatta's death, in the late summer of 1979, naïve and still confident from my recent honors and fame, I let a local official with connections to Moi convince me to approach the president for a land grant as compensation for my athletic achievements. I traveled with this official to the state house in Eldoret, where he introduced me to Moi, saying, "Mr. President, here is Henry Rono, the famous runner. I would like to request that you give him some land." Moi glanced at me with a vicious look before saying, "Kilibwoni is where he is from. The Nandis from Kilibwoni are rubbish. I have given a lot of plots to many of them, up to 3,000 acres, and they still want more." I came out of that meeting with my head hurting and realizing how easy it would be to become a target of Moi's.

In the fall of 1978, I went back to WSU. Many people asked why I would return to school when I could easily parlay my recent record-breaking performances into a professional running career with lucrative corporate sponsorships. I simply responded that I felt that a college education could offer me more. When I returned to WSU, Coach Chaplin was surprised to see me since he had heard a rumor in the news that I would be transferring to a college in Europe. Before I could even unpack, Chaplin shuttled me off to a university board meeting attended by the WSU president.

On the way to the meeting, I learned that Chaplin wanted a new track stadium and that the meeting we would be attending would decide how the university's budget would be distributed amongst the athletic programs. Coach Chaplin had written me a one-sentence appeal to the president, which could have hardly been more rudimentary. After the university president introduced me as "a legend who conquered the world of track and field in 80 days," I turned to him and recited my line: "We need a new stadium to improve our athletic program." The president answered, "Henry, we will do it." As soon as the words of approval had left the president's mouth, Chaplin motioned to me that we should leave immediately. When the president asked us to stay longer, Coach replied, "We have to get back to the track."

Soon after the meeting, Coach Chaplin took me on a fundraising tour for the new stadium, and we barnstormed through so many Washington cities and towns on a small airplane that I can hardly remember them all. After the tour, I found that my efforts had helped raise three million dollars, which would be enough to complete the construction of the stadium. The modern track facility was finished in 1979, and, since I was such a popular athlete on campus and had put so much time and effort in raising money for the stadium, there were rumors that the stadium might be named after me, which would have been a welcomed honor. Instead, they named the facility Morreburry Stadium in memory of one of Coach Chaplin's WSU predecessors.

During the cross-country season in the winter of 1978, I ran fairly well, routinely winning races until the championships, where I ended up placing second-to-last after I took a wrong turn off the course. By the time I righted myself, I went from leading the race to being so far out of contention that I decided to conserve my energy and jog to the finish line at a leisurely pace. Alberto Salazar, an up-and-coming Cuban American runner who would soon become the darling of running tabloids, ended up winning the championship. As it would turn out, it would be the only time Salazar would defeat me head to head, and, in doing so, he didn't even have the pleasure of beating me in a close, down-to-the-wire finish.

I went home to Kenya over Christmas vacation, and, when I had returned to WSU in January, I had a stack of letters of invitation from all over the world. Some were from meet directors requesting my participation in upcoming events, while others were from running organizations and publications asking me to attend ceremonies to receive various honors. One very memorable letter arrived from Moscow, where a Russian organization had named me athlete of the year. When I began making preparations to attend, Chaplin discouraged me, saying, "What would the world say if you go to Russia? They'd think you were a Communist." Naïvely heeding Chaplin's advice, I politely turned down my invitation to Moscow.

Chaplin was always wary of having his runners get tangled up in politics, which is one reason he had so many more conflicts with runners such as Kosgei, who were more politically outspoken than I. It's also the reason Chaplin had me refuse an invitation from Muhammad Ali to participate in his indoor track club. Ali so wanted me to attend and was so surprised by my rejection that he made a call to the Kenyan Embassy in Washington, DC, who then called me to try and change my mind. Someone later told me that, if necessary, Ali was prepared to call the president of Kenya himself to have *him* persuade me to participate in the track club. Unfortunately, I missed out on the opportunity to meet one of the genuine legends in all of sports history due in large part to Chaplin's insistence that I retain an apolitical image.

Against Chaplin's wishes, I traveled with Mike Kosgei to indoor meets in the United States and Canada in the winter of 1979. My decision caused Chaplin to curse Kosgei to no end with his rants of "Kosgei thinks he's taking over my coaching job! I'm going to kick his ass out of here, that son of a bitch!" In retrospect, I don't believe it was merely Kosgei's politics that irked Chaplin. While Chaplin continuously exploited me under the pretense of helping me, Kosgei, Chaplin realized, would provide me with advice and opportunities that truly would be in my best interest. For instance, Kosgei and I were planning to establish an African headquarters for Nike in Nairobi. We had begun negotiations with Nike representative Jeff Holster and would have gone through with the deal, which promised to be quite lucrative, if Nike had not made the deal contingent upon Kosgei first undergoing a stringent, pseudo-military training routine and indoctrination. Kosgei was too much of a freethinker to agree to such a stringent initiation process and so he turned down the offer, opting to finish up his degree instead. In the summer of 1979, Kosgei returned to Kenya, where he would become one of the most successful national coaches in Kenyan history. In truth, Kosgei would have been successful in whatever career path he chose, and I could just as easily envision him a successful executive at Nike as a legendary Kenyan track coach.

In the spring of 1979, the KAAA chartered a plane for Phillip Ndoo—at the time, my countryman and friend who went on to become a sportswriter and then assistant director at the IAAF—to visit WSU to convince me to run in the upcoming Jomo Kenyatta Memorial Meet, which was to be held in Kenya that summer and, after which, the KAAA intended to have me accompany Kenya's national youth track team on a tour of Europe. However, I told Ndoo that I was tired of having to mediate spats between meet directors, KAAA officials, and Kenyan athletes. I also told him that I intended to rest during the summer and get ahead in my course work so as to prepare myself for the intensive training sessions that would be required as preparation for the Moscow Olympics in 1980.

Ndoo disregarded my plans, refusing to believe that I was serious about my education and degree. When he didn't accept my reasons for turning him down, I became more assertive, telling him he was wasting my time and that I had important issues to worry about such as getting to class. Unfortunately, when I returned from class, he was still in Chaplin's office, trying to work a deal behind my back. Chaplin asked Ndoo if he could travel with me to Kenya if I decided to attend. Ndoo insisted that this would be a bad idea since having a White coach chaperone me, Kenya's best athlete, would reflect badly on the KAAA. In a strange turn of events, however, the KAAA would soon change its mind about allowing Chaplin to accompany me. While it was obvious that the KAAA was returning to its usual method of persuasion, using a friend or countryman with whom I was sympathetic to try to convince me to follow the organization's wishes, their messenger this time was in on a plan more underhanded than the previous schemes.

Later that spring, Ndoo attended the NCAA championships in Chicago, Illinois to persuade as many elite Kenyan runners as he could to participate in the Kenyatta Memorial. At one point, Ndoo was confronted by one of the most brilliant-minded athletes I know, Amos Korir, who later graduated with an MBA degree in economics from the University of Oregon. Once Korir questioned Ndoo's intentions and connection to the KAAA, Ndoo turned away and avoided him from there on out. After being ambushed by Korir, Ndoo approached me, changing his tune about allowing Chaplin to accompany me to the Kenyatta Memorial, saying that if I wanted my coach to travel with me, the KAAA would accommodate my wishes. Of course, the KAAA had not just suddenly transformed into a concerned and obliging organization.

My reason for insisting on Chaplin's accompaniment was not because I particularly enjoyed his company; in fact, his agreeing to accompany me to Kenya was most likely a sign of his desire to be an active participant in my career so as to gain more control of me and have greater access to my finances. Nonetheless, I suspected that if I went alone, the KAAA might confiscate my passport and not let me return to the United States or Europe. Having a Western coach with me as an advocate and witness would all but ensure that the KAAA wouldn't risk detaining me. My suspicions proved valid. And while I was right to believe that they wouldn't attempt to detain me with Chaplin around, they had planned to get rid of Chaplin before forcing their will upon me.

The late Kipsubai Koskei leaked Ndoo's and the KAAA's plan to grab me once I set foot in the Nairobi airport and put Chaplin on the next flight back to the United States. Eventually, Ndoo himself admitted to the plan. While I felt stabbed in the back by Ndoo, I also felt sorry for the position he was put in by the KAAA's bribery. Once Ndoo's scheme was exposed, Chaplin objected to my driving Ndoo back to the airport. I did so anyways. Ndoo couldn't believe he had failed in his mission, and, perhaps, he was afraid that there might be consequences when he returned to Kenya, for, just as I shook hands with him and said goodbye at the airport, he fainted.

While Ndoo had failed in persuading me to attend the Kenyatta Memorial, the KAAA had still not given up on me. As I proceeded to compete in international meets in Europe that summer, I was continuously harassed by Ongeri about my competition schedule. One day, he called me while I was staying in the London Skyway Hotel, saying, "President Moi said come home and run for your late friend Mzee Kenyatta and you can go anywhere you want with total freedom and no fear." With Moi's words of reassurance, along with Ongeri's word that if I attended the Kenyatta Memorial Meet he would stop meddling with my future plans and schedule, I agreed to head to Nairobi.

Initially, the Kenyan government and KAAA officials seemed to be keeping their word, giving me space before the Kenyatta Memorial Meet, in which I performed well, winning the 3,000 steeplechase. However, after the meet, Ongeri went back on his word and pestered me about supervising Kenya's youth national team on a competition tour. When I declined, an official in full military uniform told me, "You'd better listen to what we say or we will make a lot trouble for you." At this point, Isaiah Kiplagat confiscated my passport, keeping it at his home and making it impossible for me to leave the country. There was little I could do but head upcountry to stay with my family. Eventually, meet directors in Europe, such as Andrea Broker, learned of how Kiplagat confiscated my passport. When the media got hold of the story, the KAAA buckled under the bad publicity and had police officers come to my home to let me know that I could retrieve my passport at any time from Kiplagat's residence. When I arrived at Kiplagat's house, he didn't even greet me. Instead, he had his children meet me at the door. They handed me back my passport, all the while flattering me about what a great runner they thought I was. With my passport back, I headed to the airport, where Broker had chartered a private jet to escort me to Switzerland, where I would run in a meet in Zurich.

After running meets in Europe at the end of the summer, I returned to Pullman to continue work on my degree. One afternoon that fall, as I sat down in the cafeteria between my classes, a Swedish TV crew showed up unannounced to film a feature on me. The crew informed me that they had first contacted the KAAA and paid $5,000 for the rights to interview me. They said they had also contacted Coach Chaplin. I told them they should have first thought to contact me. I was tired of Chaplin and the KAAA making decisions for me behind my back and trying to control my career, and so I declined the interview. The crew asked me for their money back. I told them that I wasn't sure whether just the KAAA or the KAAA and Chaplin took their money and then asked them, "Shouldn't you ask for your money from the person who took it?"

The TV crew ended up filming Mike Kosgei. When I asked him why he agreed to the filming, he said, "They went through the trouble to travel all this distance, and I didn't want them to leave empty-handed; besides, it's not their fault that the KAAA swindled and misled them." After the incident, I was not surprised to find out that Ongeri had refused to return the money to the Swedish television station.

That fall semester was exhausting. My relationship with Coach Chaplin had become untenable, and, as I got into the advanced stages of my degree, the course work was becoming more demanding. However, I was also becoming a much more independent scholar, and my reading skills and study habits had improved dramatically since my first semester at WSU. At the end of the semester, after winning my third NCAA cross-country championship, I was exhausted and decided to head back to Kenya to tie up some loose ends and tend to some personal matters. Before the end of the year, I purchased a 100-acre farm in Molo and married Jennifer Chapkemboi, a Nandi woman I met in Kabirirsang Primary School.

In January, I toured New Zealand and Australia in preparation for the 1980 Olympics. While I was Auckland, I received a call in my hotel room at 2:00 AM from the BBC informing me that Kenya had elected to boycott the Moscow Olympics. I was disheartened beyond words and too emotional to answer the reporter's questions. Several days later, I raced the 10,000 meters in 27:31.68 in Melbourne, just 9.28 seconds off my world record, proving that my progress would have been right on schedule to give me a chance to medal in that year's Olympics. But what could I do? I was helpless against the boycott. After racing in a number of indoor competitions in Canada and the United States, I returned to Kenya. When I arrived at Jomo Kenyatta Airport, the airport employees expressed their sorrow for me. They also told me that Muhammad Ali had recently visited Nairobi to persuade the Kenyan government to take part in the American Olympic boycott. "We got a hell of a lot of money from the U.S. government," one of the airport porters told me. I headed straight from the airport to my farm in Molo to be with my family.

Poster commemorating my four world records in 81 days in 1978.

My mother, Chemaiyo, and grandmother, Kobotkimisik.

President Kenyatta and I at the statehouse in 1978 after he presented me with the Order of the Burning Spear.

Setting a world record in the 5,000 meters on April 8, 1978 in Berkeley, California, the first of my four world records in the span of 81 days.

Alone at the finish line.

Setting a world record in the 3,000-steeplechase on May 13, 1978 in Seattle, Washington, the second of my four world records in 81 days.

Sitting in the bleachers before a meet in Pullman, Washington in 1978.

Competing in the steeplechase in the 1978 Commonwealth Games.

Setting a world record in the 10,000 meters on June 11, 1978 in Vienna, Austria—the third of my four world records in 81 days.

Winning a 5,000-meter race in London in June of 1978.

Setting a world record in the in the 3,000 meters on June 27, 1978 in Oslo, Norway, the final of my four world records in 81 days.

Taking my victory lap in Oslo after setting my fourth world record.

Above the water in the steeplechase at the 1978 Commonwealth Games.

Clearing the water in the steeplechase at the 1978 Commonwealth Games.

Crossing the finish line in the 5,000 meters at the 1978 Commonwealth Games.

Breaking my own world record in the 5,000 meters in Knarvik, Norway, September 13, 1981.

Victory lap after setting 5,000-meter world record in Knarvik, Norway.

IAAF official pulling me from the starting line on June 26, 1982 in Oslo, Norway.

Edging out Alberto Salazar in the 10,000 meters at his own promotional meet on April 8, 1982 at Hayward Field in Eugene, Oregon.

My shoulders buckling in disbelief after being escorted from the track by police officers in Oslo.

Falsely arrested in New Jersey on November 16, 1986.

Pastor Billy Karanja blessing the remains of one of the workers slain in the raid on my farm in Molo, April of 1992.

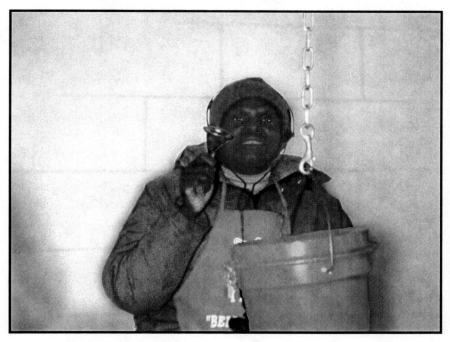

Working for the Salvation Army in Salt Lake City in December of 1992.

The Albuquerque Valley High School Vikings 1997 girls' cross-country team, for whom I was an assistant coach. Jaramillo, the head coach, is on the far right.

Working at a carwash in Portland, Oregon in 1995.

Chapter XV
A Downward Spiral

Dispirited by the boycott, my usual near-religious training routine started to lose steam, and soon my weight began to creep up. Ever since I was a kid, I was ridiculed for my round body type and weight and had to run every morning and evening just to make myself look like a runner. In June 1980, during my honeymoon in Nairobi, I received a call to my hotel room from my on-again, off-again agent, Gordon Cooper, who urged me to return to the United States for the upcoming pre-Olympic summer meets. A $20,000 advance and a seat on a Concorde from London to New York enticed me into taking the offer. Cooper met me at JFK Airport and rushed me to the first meet within six hours of my arrival. A fatigued and visibly overweight world record holder,

I treated the spectators to a major surprise by placing dead last in the race.

After a heated confrontation with Cooper, I headed to New Mexico to join a number of my running friends who lived and trained in the foothills and mountains above Albuquerque. Cooper trailed me to Albuquerque and appeared at the doorstep of my rented room accompanied by a heavily muscled and tattooed strongman. Cooper asked for my passport, and I felt like I had no choice but to give it to him. Then he demanded that I return the $20,000 he had paid me to compete in the meet I finished last in. Fortunately, Nike loaned me the money to pay off Cooper, who promptly returned my passport.

With my passport back, I left for Europe to run the 5,000 meters in Stockholm and then Oslo. I ran respectably in both meets, though I was still a far cry from my world-record form. With the Olympics getting ready to commence, I returned to my farm in Molo, where I watched the track-and-field competitions on television from my home. I was dejected and had the feeling that my running career had just passed right before my eyes.

After the Olympics, I returned to the United States to run in road races with fellow Kenyan Abraham Hussein, whom I lived with for a time late that summer in Albuquerque before returning with him to Kenya that fall. While road races weren't exactly lucrative in those days, several hundred dollars per race kept me financially afloat through the rest of the year.

In January of 1981, I returned to Pullman to finish my Bachelor of Education Degree. At this time, I was becoming more assertive with Coach Chaplin, making certain that his plans for my running career didn't come between me and graduation. For instance, as soon as I arrived on campus, I had him sign my financial aid paperwork. Only after this paperwork had been processed and my aid approved did I tell Chaplin that I wouldn't be running for him that spring as I would be opting instead to focus full time on my studies. Chaplin tried long and hard to persuade me to run that spring, acting pitiful and trying to make me feel guilty for abandoning him. However, I stood fast, keeping focused on completing my degree.

Chapter XVI
The Most Meteoric Comeback in Track History

That June, after I graduated and Chaplin no longer had any leverage in his relationship with me, I returned to his office to talk about my professional running prospects. He told me that meet directors wouldn't have me in their meets that summer since I hadn't been training. "You've just been here drinking," he told me. I told him I had actually been busy finishing up my degree. I later found that he had told meet directors throughout Europe that I was out of shape. Although I didn't feel it was his place to dissuade meet directors from approaching me, for once Chaplin was right: I was sorely out of shape.

Nonetheless, I tried my best to persuade meet directors in Europe to enter me in their events that summer, even though when

I showed up at the track, my beer belly was protruding from my workout top. "Your coach said you had retired," one meet director told me. Another wanted me to return to Kenya to train for six months and then contact him about the possibility of competing in Europe the following season.

Stubborn as I was, I tossed around Europe all through June, loitering at various meets. Eventually, I convinced a Finnish meet director to let me compete in the 5,000 meters at his meet. The result was even worse than I could have imagined as I was lapped two and a half times by the winner. It was the poorest performance of my career, and the meet director was infuriated. After this debacle at the Finnish meet, virtually no other meet directors were even willing to talk to me.

In July, I headed to Germany to train in the forest hills of Cologne, where I enjoyed the rainy season, running through densely forested paths as steam rose in front of me from evaporating dew and the moisture on the leaves from the previous night's rain. Training in relative isolation in the German forest allowed me to center my mind, and soon my body followed suit.

In August, I snuck into an event in Zurich and tried to convince Andrea Broker to let me race. He gave me a number for the 'B' race. I refused and entered myself into the elite race, where I placed fifth. While it was a far cry from my record-breaking performances of three years past, the performance was equally far removed from my pathetic showing just weeks earlier at the meet in Finland. Broker was pleasantly surprised by my performance that day, and soon word of my comeback began to circulate among meet directors.

After the Zurich meet, I went to Berlin and placed second in a 3,000-meter race. After this performance, the meet directors were convinced of my return and were once again covetous of my presence in their meets. Soon, I had tickets waiting for me to fly to any event in Europe. In Cologne, I ran the 5,000 meters in 13:22, finishing a half-second behind the winner. Once I saw my 5,000 time in Cologne, I became attune to the steep incline of my progress and confident that, within a race or two, I would be able to post the year's best time in the 5,000. Two days later in Germany, I ran a season's best 13:12 in the 5,000. The press started buzzing over what they were calling one of the most meteoric comebacks in track history. Only weeks earlier, I had a beer gut and was lapped two and a half times in a 5,000 meter race; now I had claimed the season's best time in that same distance and felt ready to claim a world record or maybe two. The German sportswriter Robert Hartman proclaimed, "He is crazy. How could he comeback in only two months?" For the rest of the European season, I was running by myself unchallenged, competing solely against the times of the records I sought.

I went to Brussels, Belgium and ran the 10,000 for another season's best time, almost lapping the runner up. In a German meet, I ran the 3,000 meters in 7:40, yet another year's-best time. My shape and confidence were both cresting, and I felt the time was right to claim a world record in the 10,000 meters. At this time, KAAA and other African sports officials were courting me to run for the African team in the 1981 World Championship in Rome. I told them I would on one condition: I get to compete in the 10,000 meters. They agreed.

Once I got to Rome, however, the African sports officials had suddenly changed their minds, deciding that Ethiopian Maruss Hiffter, who was slotted to be Africa's representative in the 10,000 meters before my rapid comeback, should run the event instead of me. Robert Hartman, the journalist who only weeks earlier had sung the praises of my comeback, was now lobbying to have me excluded from the Rome meet, writing that Hiffter was more deserving to run in the 10,000 meters since he had been training with the African team all along. A Ugandan official repeated Hartman's sentiment, saying that all African runners should be treated fairly and that I shouldn't get preferential treatment simply because I had been running well recently. I was furious as I knew that the World Championships were perfectly timed for me to claim the 10,000-meter world record in Rome.

Realizing how upset I was at being denied my chance to run in the 10,000 meters, Kiplagat, Boit, and Ongeri came to my hotel room to try and calm me down. Kiplagat offered me a payoff to not stir up controversy in the media. I refused as my eyes were entirely locked on one thing: world records. Later, Robert Hartman also came to my room to console me. I told him I felt I could have done something truly historic in the 10,000 meters had he and African officials not interfered. To me, it was not only my loss, but a loss to any person who was a track aficionado as Hartman claimed to be. After an East German runner won the 10,000 meters, Hartman's hidden motives for encouraging African officials to keep me out of the race came to light and made the African officials look foolish.

Before the 10,000-meter race, I left Rome as I was unable to stomach the thought of witnessing the race in which I felt I would have claimed a world record, and I competed in a 5,000-meter race in Rieti, Italy. While I still felt like I was in good form, I had been preparing for the 10,000 meters and, disappointingly, I only placed second in the 5,000. I then headed to London, where I ran a 5,000-meter race in an impressive 13:12. Since I was still running at peak form and my best opportunity to break the 10,000-meter race had passed, I figured I'd better take advantage of my recent surge to claim any world record I could. I told a Norwegian meet director that I was ready to run a world-record 5,000 meters. It would cost him $7,500 to have me in his race, which was a lot of money in those days, but he agreed.

On September 13, 1981, I knocked 2.2 seconds off of the 5,000-meter world record. It was the last race of the season, and I was elated to have finished on such a high note. Journalists, meet directors, and other runners agreed: the sleeping lion of the running world had awoken. It was impossible for them to fathom that, in only three months, I had gone from being lapped two and a half times in the 5,000 meters to claiming a world record in that same event.

Chapter XVII
Trouble on Molo Farm

I returned to Kenya still beaming from my comeback and fifth world record. When I became disillusioned waiting for the Kenyan government to fulfill its promises to award my accomplishments with a gift of land, I decided to buy my own property in Molo. While I was moving my family from Kapsabet to Molo, I heard that an Australian meet director was in Nairobi looking for me so as to convince me to run in the pre-Commonwealth Games in Brisbane. I went to Australia, won a 5,000-meter race, and then flew to Pullman, where I would spend the fall semester working on a second degree and assisting Coach Chaplin in training new recruits.

During winter break, I returned to Molo, where I enjoyed a pleasant Christmas with my family on our new farm. On

Christmas afternoon, while I was walking outside my house, I saw two people nearing my property. When I approached them, I learned they were President Moi's security guards. My neighbor, Nge'ny, a high-ranking official in the current regime, was having a Christmas gathering for President Moi, who had presented him with property adjacent to my farm. The security guards asked if I was Kip Keino, since by my late twenties, I had started to resemble my hero. I told them who I was, and they invited me to enter onto my neighbor's property, saying, "You might recognize some friends there." As I walked past the crowd that had gathered around the sheep slaughtered for the celebration, I saw President Moi exit Nge'ny's house and walk to where his property bordered mine. They looked over my land, with Nge'ny pointing to particular parts of my land, as if to illustrate to Moi where he would like to extend his property. It was only a coincidence that I had purchased property where Moi had been awarding land to his cronies, and, since Moi had not given me my land, he had no legal power to reallocate any part of it.

  The following evening, December 26, at about 6:00 PM, Nge'ny came to my farm to talk to me about my property, wondering how I got my hands on such rich farmland. My land was much lusher than my neighbor's, plus it had a stream running through it, while Nge'ny's farm had no watercourse. "Where does someone like you get the money to buy a lot of land as nice as yours?" Nge'ny asked me. His questions were beginning to take on the tone of interrogation. "My 100 acres were given to me by Mzee Moi," Nge'ny told me, as if to prove a point. Then Nge'ny asked if I had a receipt for my property, and I told him of course I did. He then offered me a proposition, saying, "I know you have done a lot of work on your land, a lot of development." He hesitated for a moment and then continued, "But I could give you 150 acres in Kitale that could compensate."

To try to lay Nge'ny's ambitions on my land to rest, I tried to convince him that I had connections to Moi. I said that Moi had promised me 25 acres in Uasin, Gishu, but I had been so busy traveling to competitions and finishing up my degree that I had not had the opportunity to take the president up on his offer. In those days, if you were a well-known individual, you had to have some tangible connection to the president, otherwise other influential people, such as my neighbor, who was a district postmaster, could easily exploit your lack of connection to the ruling party. By the time my neighbor left that evening, I had some foresight into the difficulties he would create for my family and me if we didn't submit to his wishes by giving him our land. Still, I was prepared to stand up for the property, which I had purchased myself and had every legal right to. However, I couldn't have foreseen just how persistent and extreme my neighbor's tactics of persuasion would be, as I suspect they eventually culminated in the destruction of my farm, the plundering of my livestock, and the murder of two of my workers in 1992.

Chapter XVIII
Cooper and Mibey

In the spring of 1982, I returned to Pullman to continue work on my second degree. One afternoon, I was drinking pitchers of beer at my customary evening hangout, Cougar Cottage, when James Mibey, a fellow Kenyan and wannabe runner whom I considered to be a casual friend, burst into the bar and grabbed me, saying we had to leave now. He told me to get in the car and not to ask any questions. Then he asked me where I lived. When we came to my house, however, he accelerated past it and rushed me to a hotel where Gordon Cooper was waiting. Needless to say, I was alarmed since I had a long history of disputes with Cooper over his handling of my running affairs when he was my agent. Cooper had used scare tactics to take advantage of me in the past, such as the time when he followed me to Albuquerque the previous summer with a strongman and demanded I return the $20,000 he paid me to compete in a race in which I finished last. When I spoke to Cooper in his hotel room, however, he was calm and even complimentary of my running success in Europe the previous summer. After a long span of small talk, he had Mibey drive me home.

On the drive to my house, I tried to figure out what Mibey's connection to Cooper was. Unfortunately, it would take me years to realize that Mibey was a simple conman hired by Cooper to keep an eye on me and persuade me to make the choices for my career that Cooper deemed most profitable. It was the same paradigm that the KAAA had long used to gain influence with me, sending a countryman whom I considered a friend to try and influence me into doing things I didn't care to do. Still naïve to Mibey's motives, I dismissed his connection to Cooper and even became his roommate in the summer of 1982 and again in 1983.

While living with Mibey in Eugene, Oregon, I stopped receiving important letters and packages and later realized Mibey had been opening and confiscating my mail. I don't know whether his intention was to spy on my personal affairs or to steal from me and try to infiltrate my bank accounts. When I questioned him about my suspicions, he began praising my running accomplishments and then went on to talk about what a good Christian he was. If he really felt pressured, he would mention his allegiance to President Moi, whom he claimed to have some connection to and whom he knew was upset with my lack of submissiveness to the KAAA.

Cooper wanted a number of things from me. For one, he wanted me to switch my sponsorship allegiances from Nike to Adidas. I figured that he must have had a deal with Adidas executives that promised him a healthy paycheck if he could get me to leave Nike. Cooper also had a vested interest in my career, though it was certainly a selfish financial interest that had little or nothing to do with any genuine concern about my well-being. Cooper was critical of my decision to not only finish up my degree at WSU, but he was especially hostile about my pursuing a second bachelor degree and my talk of seeking a graduate-level degree with the hopes of becoming a teacher. "If Henry is so interested in a degree, we can buy him one," Cooper would sometimes say. At his core, Cooper was a cold-hearted businessman, and he could not understand how I could be so indifferent to the fortunes he promised me if I would only cooperate with his plans for my career.

Cooper felt that American track coaches who recruited Kenyan runners were doing these athletes a disservice, robbing them of the four years of appearance fees and corporate sponsorships that turning professional could afford them. It was Cooper's opinion that few Kenyan runners could actually benefit from an education at an American university since many came from limited formal educational backgrounds, and some, like me, had only the equivalent of a primary education. Of course, Cooper's impression that Kenyan runners attending college cared nothing about their educations was false. Certainly, there were Kenyan runners who emphasized their training over school, just as there were American runners who did so. However, most of the Kenyan runners of whom I was a teammate cared deeply about their educations, and many parlayed their degrees into greater professional success off the track than on it.

When I now reflect on Mibey's insistence that I give up my educational aspirations to focus on my running pursuits, as well as on Chaplin's insistence during my days at WSU that I remain in college to finish my education, I realize that while both their motives were primarily selfish, each probably thought he was doing me a favor in the long run, which allowed each to rationalize exploiting and manipulating me in the short term.

When Cooper had Mibey nab me from Cougar Cottage in January of 1982, I was not only in the process of finishing my second degree, but also helping Coach Chaplin with his new recruits, many of whom were Kenyan runners who wanted to attend the same university I had. Cooper was using Mibey as an intermediary to try and convince me to encourage the new Kenyan recruits to drop out of school and sign with him. While this seemed to be Cooper's most immediate goal for Mibey, his more general responsibility was to keep close tabs on me, making sure I wasn't drinking excessively and that I was on track with my training for the '84 Olympics. Though Mibey's foremost responsibility was to work as a pawn for Cooper, I sometimes suspected he was also working for Kenyan officials, keeping an eye on me and also trying to influence me to make professional decisions agreeable to their desires for my running career. I base this suspicion not only on the fact that Mibey would always drop President Moi's name to intimidate me whenever I would question him or buck his influence, but also on the fact that he was later hired by the Moi regime as a district officer, which was a position that required him, among other things, to terrorize those who questioned or rebuked government authority.

Unfortunately for Cooper, Mibey was a poor choice for a chaperone as he was a conman and a gigolo who enjoyed the nightlife and had aspirations for fame—whether it be as an athlete or a movie star—but no specific plan on how to attain it. Often times Mibey would go to nightclubs trying to impress people, especially women, by telling them that he was an Olympic medallist—a claim that seemed credible considering he was keeping my company. At other times, since he had studied communications while trying to break into the track program at the University of Utah, he claimed to be a sportswriter. But all Mibey ever amounted to was a world-class name-dropper, and he used his connection to me to open a number of social opportunities for himself that otherwise would not have existed.

Years later, I would find out that Cooper blamed Mibey for sabotaging my aspirations for the '84 Olympics. Cooper felt that Mibey's fast lifestyle enabled my drinking and deterred my training. While living with Mibey was certainly harmful to me psychologically, he was only one of many people involved in my life and affairs at the time leading up to the '84 Olympics, including Chaplin, various KAAA officials, Nge'ny, and not to mention Cooper himself, who contributed to the psychological breakdown that lead to my leaving the United States for Europe, giving up my training regimen, later returning to Kenya, and finally falling deeply into alcoholism. Once it was clear that my chances to run—much less win gold in Los Angeles—were past, Mibey all but disappeared from my life, as did the specter of Cooper... well, at least for a few years, until the 1988 Seoul Olympics were approaching and Cooper, with the help of Mibey, would attempt once again to take control of my personal life and career, trying to force me to train for the Olympics so that he might reap financial opportunities from my gold-medal prospects.

Chapter XIX
The Most Memorable Race I Ever Ran

When I picked up the phone on March 8, 1982 to hear the voice of Alberto Salazar—the talented, charismatic, and good looking Cuban American runner who was currently the golden child of the American running world and of Nike—I knew exactly what he needed from me.

It had recently been in the sports reports that Nike made an agreement with Salazar: if he could organize a series of middle-distance races, ranging from 3,000 to 10,000 meters, against the world's premier runners and not only win each of these events, but break American records in the process, the company would reward him by making him the first single-season millionaire in track-and-field history. However, Nike had one more stipulation: the current world-record holder in the 10,000 meters, Henry Rono, must run in that event, which was the first on Salazar's schedule. Since the series of races was Salazar's brainchild, Nike gave him the responsibility of recruiting runners for his events. As a result, not only did Salazar have to train vigorously for his attempt to claim an improbable string of middle-distance victories, but he would have to do so while dealing with the emotional stress and responsibilities of being a meet director.

When Salazar called me, we both knew I was out of shape. In fact, I wondered whether it was his intention to wait as long as possible before inviting me to his meet so as to give me less of an opportunity to prepare for the race and therefore less of a chance to overshadow him in his own event. Throughout the spring semester, my mind was preoccupied with my studies as I was striving for my second bachelor's degree, as well as with assisting Chaplin in training his new recruits. I had no intention of running in an elite race in the near future, and so my training had been casual at best. Sensing my lack of enthusiasm for the race, Salazar reminded me that just three-and-a-half years ago, I had broken world records in four events, including the event he was asking me to run in, the 10,000 meters. "But that was a long time ago," I told him, "And it took me a great deal of time and preparation to get into shape to break those records." Salazar told me not to worry; I had four weeks until the

April 8 meet, which would be run in Eugene, Oregon. Furthermore, Salazar said he didn't expect me to contend, but to simply finish in a respectable time... say under 28 minutes. "I am sure you can run the 10,000 in 27:58 four weeks from now," Salazar reassured me, "And if you do, I'll pay you $2,000."

Salazar scheduled me for a number of minor 5,000-meter races leading up to the showdown on April 8. First, I went to Walla Walla, Washington, where I ran a mediocre 13:53. Realizing how far out of shape I was, I intensified my training, and, when I ran in a meet in California two weeks later, I had cut an impressive 16 seconds off of my time in Walla Walla, finishing in 13:37. I was cautiously optimistic about my prospects. If somehow I could continue to gain momentum during my final week of training, maybe, just maybe I might have an outside chance at giving Salazar a race.

In the week leading up to the meet, Salazar phoned me numerous times at my training camp in Salt Lake City, making sure that I still intended to attend. I could sense his anxiety and began to realize that the stress of organizing the race might be taking its toll on him. Perhaps I was out of shape physically, but Salazar would potentially be emotionally exhausted and thus out of shape mentally. With five days left, I further increased the intensity of my training routine, emphasizing daily interval workouts instead of easing into the event as I usually would with long, even-paced runs intended solely to maintain my shape and weight. By increasing the intensity of my training all the way up to the day before the event, I was risking the possibility of fatigue and soreness during the race; however, such drastic training measures were necessary in order to give me any chance of improving my time into the range necessary to compete with Salazar.

Early in the morning on the day before the race, I flew into Eugene, Oregon. Salazar welcomed me to a banquet he had prepared, where the press hounded me about the shape I was in, asking how I intended to go from placing second amid a mediocre field in the 5,000 meters the week before to contending with Salazar. After the banquet was over, the athletes were handed their racing numbers. When mine was nowhere to be found, I was told to go and ask Salazar for it.

Salazar told me he had my number, but that we'd have to walk to the track complex to get it. When we got there, we walked out to the center of the track, and we both looked around wistfully, sharing the kind of uneasy camaraderie that only two elite athletes—whose respect for one another is only rivaled by the desire to defeat the other—can share. He handed me the number 101 and pins. He told me my hotel was not far from the track and that he'd like to walk me to my room. On the walk back to my hotel, Salazar still seemed uneasy, apparently worrying about whether I might pull out of tomorrow's big race. "So you're really going to show up tomorrow right?" he asked, "Now you know how to get to the track from your hotel. Remember, the race is at 2:00 PM, and you should arrive an hour early." I put up one finger and asked just to be sure, "1:00 PM?" When he had walked me to my hotel, he said he had to return to the banquet to tie up a few loose ends concerning the meet. Still, he must have regarded me as his greatest loose end, fearing that if I didn't show up to his race, the entire event—as well as all his aspirations to break every major American middle-distance record in succession and become the first one-year millionaire in track-and-field history—would unravel.

My strenuous training during the week leading up to the race and the rapid improvements in my running times that accompanied it boosted my confidence; however, my body was sore and my muscles tight, especially my hamstrings. While I was in peak mental condition and less-than-ideal physical shape, Salazar was the inverse. He could hardly have been in better physical condition for the race; however, his commitments to organizing and directing the meet had stretched his mind and emotions thin. I realized that if I were to beat him the next morning, I would have to run a smart race. I wasn't in the shape Salazar was, and, if he ran a smarter race than I, I would have little chance to defeat him.

Before the race, I went for my usual early morning run, jogging through the woods of Eugene, invigorated by the sharp spring breeze. In the woods, I found a small hill with a moderate incline and climbed it repeatedly with increasing intensity and almost complete abandon for 45 minutes, as though I didn't have a race to save myself for that day. As I ran back to my motel, I realized the tightness I had felt the previous days had left me. This was a very good sign, and it boosted my confidence over my prospects in the afternoon's race even more.

At the motel, I started envisioning how I would approach the race. I knew I couldn't win a sprint with Salazar, so I would have to pace myself and hope he didn't start the race at a break-all speed and pull away too soon. If I could keep his pace early on, I was confident that my mental strength and experience would allow me to outlast him. Before I left the hotel, I envisioned my ideal finish to the race, with me outlasting Salazar down the stretch and edging him out by a lunge.

When I arrived at the stadium at 1:00 PM sharp, Salazar looked relieved. There were races going on leading up to the main event. Salazar and I watched the 5K together, and he was happy with the winner's time of 13:30. There was a slight drizzle, and the air was cool. Sportswriters like to make a big deal about how American runners thrive in cold and wet weather while African runners struggle in such conditions. However, my career at WSU should have dispelled such myths as I won meets in freezing, snowy conditions as well as in hot and sunny weather.

Soon, the introductions were underway. I was the final runner introduced, and, when my name was announced over the PA system, the whole stadium came alive with at least as much excitement as when Salazar had been introduced. I glanced up at the crowd, acknowledging their applause ever so briefly before hurrying to the starting line.

From the starter's pistol, Salazar set out at brisk pace, much faster than I would have liked. After a few laps, Salazar and I were cranking along at an unbelievable pace, along with four other runners who alternately took the lead from us. I was concerned that the 6.2-mile race would be too long for me to maintain such speed considering the shape I was in, and, if Salazar increased the pace and tried to test the explosiveness in my legs, my chances of winning would be all but finished. Still, the first mile went easily for me, and I didn't feel any pain as I heard the announcer call out the time of 4:27, which was a pace conducive to Salazar's challenging the American record.

After the first mile, Salazar and I pulled away from the pack. Fortunately for me, his pace had lessened, which allowed me to stay with him and finish the second mile in less than nine minutes. While the world record looked to be difficult to reach at that point, the American record was still within Salazar's sights. Between the second mile and the race's halfway mark, which we passed at 13:45 (keeping Salazar's hopes for the American record alive), the pace remained consistent. Salazar's running style was graceful, his leg kicks low and his stride long, which made it easy for me to draft off of him without worrying about his back kick. Salazar liked to run evenly paced races, scarcely attempting to intimidate or test his competition by mixing up his pace or surging.

Surging is a strategy that I often employed in race, and, while I was in no kind of shape to test Salazar with a surge that day, had he tested me in this way, kicking up the gear intermittently and trying to surge ahead, he could easily have left me. Because my muscles were fatigued from my unusually strenuous training leading up to the race, I would have found it difficult to find the explosive kick necessary to catch up. Perhaps Salazar figured my lack of preparation for the race would leave me fatigued as we approached the final few laps and that I would naturally slough away from his lead without his having to shake me through surging. If this is what he thought, he was wrong.

With a third of the race remaining, Salazar and I had put 100 meters between us and the rest of the field, and it was clear to the crowd, which was growing louder with each of our strides, that the race would go down to the wire, like a classic heavyweight bout between two grizzled champions slugging it out toe to toe in the final round. With one and a half laps remaining, it seemed as though Salazar had given up on the American record, which was fortunate for me, since I was afraid that if we closed in on the finish line and Salazar could smell the record, he might finally surge and be able to outlast my fatigued hamstrings.

When Salazar and I came down along the straightaway toward the starting line on our penultimate lap, the bell signaling the final lap rang out, and the crowd rose to its feet cheering with absolute abandon. Salazar was still leading, but I was closing the little distance that remained between us. With 200 meters left, I came up alongside Salazar, running shoulder-to-shoulder with him for a few seconds before taking a tenuous lead. With 100 meters left, I put my right hand up to signal to the crowd that I had the strength to finish Salazar off. With 25 meters left, I finally made my surge, for which Salazar had no answer.

I beat Salazar by one tenth of a second and was rewarded with one of the heartiest ovations I ever received. I now consider that race to be the most memorable and exhilarating victory of my running career. In the days and months following my victory, the sports pages and major track publications touted the outcome as one of the closest and thrilling finishes ever in a major track-and-field race.

After the race, I had mixed feelings about Salazar. On one hand, I commended the man for running a remarkable race just shy of the American record he was pursuing, averaging a remarkable 66 seconds per lap over 25 laps. However, I also felt that Salazar squandered his chance at an American record and victory over me by diverting so much of the energy he should have devoted to mentally preparing for the race into the stress of organizing and directing the meet. Still, he almost did what he set out to do, just missing out on the American record and a victory over me. There's no way that I could have made such an impressive showing with so much stress and so many distractions infringing upon my mental preparations for a race. My victory over Salazar proves that, among elite runners, mental preparations supersede physical training. I was in less-than-ideal physical shape and in formidable mental shape leading up to my showdown with Salazar, while he was in peak physical shape and mentally distracted.

In retrospect, I am thankful to Salazar for the opportunity he gave me to race him in such a high-profile event. I am also thankful that he agreed to sponsor my training for two months in 1989 when I was having a hard time staying sober and making ends meet. Still, my victory over Salazar in the spring of 1982 is all the sweeter since he has since made some condescending comments towards me in track-and-field publications about how my hardships in life resulted from my not taking my education seriously. While Salazar was a stellar student at Oregon and parlayed his degree into financial success as an executive at Nike, his comments about my education glossed over the differences in the circumstances leading up to our college years. While I had no education beyond primary school in Kenya, Salazar was an affluent Cuban American who received a first-rate New England high school education. I am not saying that Salazar was not a good student or that he is not a savvy and intelligent businessman worthy of his fortunes at Nike. I am only defending the earnestness with which I approached my education. Though I may not have been the college student Salazar was, I had to overcome a great deal to achieve what I was able to accomplish in college, including a cumulative GPA of over 3.0 and two separate bachelor's degrees—one in general education and the other in psychology. In my push toward the second of these degrees, I passed nine classes in a single semester.

In a September 3, 1995 article from the *Sunday Oregonian*, Salazar was quoted as saying, "The difference between [Rono] and me is that I got an education… how good he could have been is scary." In response to this remark, I would simply like to say that I have used my two bachelor's degrees to become a teacher and pursue my master's; though I could possibly have extended my reign as the greatest runner in the world had I not turned to drink, that doesn't keep me up at night. Had I never become a teacher, however, then I would really have to answer to myself and others for wasting my talents.

Chapter XX
A Dark Time

After I defeated Salazar in his own event, Nike realized my potential to claim gold at the 1984 Los Angeles Olympics, and so they signed me to a three-year contract, which would pay me $50,000 in 1982, $60,000 in 1983, and $70,000 in 1984. In the summer of 1982, after I had defeated Peter Koech and Salazar in a 5,000-meter race in Stockholm, Nike paid me the $50,000 sum of my contract's first year in full, and I promptly opened up an account in France and deposited the money in it.

At this point, things were looking up for me. Though the specters of Cooper and Mibey, my neighbor, Nge'ny, and not to mention a variety of KAAA officials still lingered in the periphery, my career for once seemed stable. I was a newlywed with a nice plot of farmland and a budding trucking business in Kenya and I was finally translating my past world records into a lucrative professional running career, replete with sizable corporate sponsorships and hefty appearance fees. Unfortunately, this time of prosperity and relative peace would be short-lived as the KAAA once again began meddling in my running career.

In June 1982, at a meet in Oslo, Norwegian police officers pulled me from the starting line. It was the most humiliating incident in my life as I went from being passionately applauded by the large crowd to being handled like a criminal in front of the same fans who had watched me break the 3,000-meter world record only four years before. I later learned that the KAAA had sent a letter to the IAAF to stop me from competing in any more meets in Europe until I submitted myself to the KAAA's jurisdiction. The KAAA officials did this under the pretense that they were taking greater control of runners' careers in order to better manage their finances and invest in their futures by putting away large amounts of their earnings in savings accounts. The KAAA, having usurped my will by colluding with the IAAF, left me with no choice but to return to Kenya where, dejected, I stayed with my family on my farm in Molo.

Soon after my return, my wife received a call from Ongeri saying that President Moi was in Nairobi and wanted to see me. My wife got nervous and started feeling uncomfortable about the message. She told me to please go promptly and do whatever Ongeri asked of me. In Nairobi, I met with the Kenyan Minister of Sports, Ole Tip Tip, and our discussion proved uneventful. Ole Tip Tip had flown back to Nairobi from the Commonwealth Games in Australia, where the rest of the Kenyan team was preparing to compete. It seems that he was receiving flack from the press for leaving me home during the Commonwealth Games and had returned to Kenya to face the music. In truth, I had refused to represent Kenya in the games as a way to buck the control the KAAA was trying to exert over my career.

Soon after my meeting with Ole Tip Tip, word came to my farm that I shouldn't hang around there long. The best thing to do, according to what people in the know were telling me, was to leave the country before the Kenyan team got home. There were rumors that since I refused to represent Kenya in the Commonwealth Games, I was going to lose my passport as soon as KAAA officials returned from Australia. I waited until the team arrived in Nairobi, briefly welcomed them, and then promptly left the country for Pullman.

In June 1983, Dave Fleming delivered me my paycheck for the second year of my contract with Nike. I sent most of the money from the first year of my contract home to my family, who used the money not only for daily expenses, but to make improvements on the farm. With the money for the second year of my contract, I intended to buy a house in Eugene. While the second year of my contract had promised me $60,000, the check Fleming handed me was only made out for $50,000. When I asked Fleming where the other $10,000 had gone, he handed me a telephone and told me to ask Coach Chaplin. On the phone, I asked Chaplin why he had Nike pay him $10,000 from my contract. Chaplin acted flustered and frustrated and went from being speechless on the phone to threatening my life. After my attempts to get a rational explanation from Chaplin failed, I handed the phone to Fleming, who told Chaplin that I intended to use the money to buy a house in Eugene.

While my contract with Nike was supposed to last through the Olympic year of 1984, due to the controversy between Chaplin and me, Nike voided the last year of my contract and reneged on the final installment of $70,000. I felt entirely exploited by Chaplin and abandoned by Nike. After all, I had negotiated the contract myself with top Nike executives and in no way had I given them permission to give any of my money directly to Chaplin.

Though I only received $50,000 dollars from Nike and the house I intended to buy in Eugene was worth $55,000, I had enough money in my French savings account to pay the difference and buy the house outright. When Chaplin learned of my plans to buy a house in Eugene, he became very upset with me, saying, "What are Kenyans going to say about your buying a home in the United States?" He tried to convince me that I didn't have the right to buy a home in the United States. Chaplin was not the only one trying to dissuade me from buying the house. Gordon Cooper echoed Chaplin's sentiment, saying that Americans wouldn't want a Kenyan living next to them, disrupting their nice, homogenous neighborhood. They would be afraid I might break into their houses or beat their kids, he said.

Though I had the money to pay for the house in cash, mysteriously, the real estate company returned my down payment and said they would be unable to complete the transaction. I later heard rumors that Chaplin had been speaking to my real estate agent, trying to convince him not to sell me the house. As with many of the injustices I suffered around this time in my life, I now realize that I had the right to pursue legal action for such matters. Still, I also realize that the American courts would probably not have been very sympathetic to a Nandi like me, with his two bottom front teeth missing, his dark skin, and his Swahili accent.

Since I was not allowed to buy the house I wanted in Eugene, I rented an apartment across the street from Mike Boit's three-bedroom house, which, strangely, he had no problem buying. John Otsyula, a very socially astute and intelligent Kenyan graduate student in chemistry at the University of Oregon, became my roommate. Otsyula became one of my dearest friends and biggest advocates. He was keen to how exploitative the people who surrounded me were.

"Your independence is a great threat to both coaches and meet directors in the United States as well as officials back home in Kenya. They want to destabilize you so that you are more vulnerable and impressionable," Otsyula told me.

Beyond all of Otsyula's sound advice, the best thing about living with him was that he worked as an amulet against Mibey, who was obviously threatened by Otsyula's intellect and outspokenness and must have realized that Otsyula had exposed him as a fraud.

Though Otsyula served as the kind of reliable friend and confidant I lacked in previous years, I still felt unstable and uprooted. Ever since the Oslo incident, I felt depressed, as though I had no control over my own professional career. Beyond that, I felt unsafe returning to Kenya. I was also beginning to internalize the sentiments of Cooper and Chaplin and came to think of myself as an outsider who would never be accepted or understood in the United States. In addition to all of this, the trucking business I had invested in a couple of years earlier was going under. I felt I had nowhere to turn, and, as a result, my passion for running was depleted. I started to rely more heavily on alcohol to soothe my damaged emotions and nerves and to get me through my long, dark nights of the soul. Over time, my depression deepened, and my alcoholism became increasingly severe until, in 1984, I stopped running all together.

By the summer of 1984, my depression and alcoholism had taken a vast toll on me, and I was in no shape—mentally, emotionally, and certainly not physically—to even compete for a spot in the Los Angeles Olympics. Tired of my stagnancy in Eugene and wanting to get away from the Olympic hoopla that was beginning to take place just down the coast in Los Angeles, I decided to travel to Europe with John Otsyula. John and I visited Germany, where I always felt welcome, and soon I felt a little better about life. Though I had no desire to run, I still had enough money left from the remainder of my Nike contract to purchase a house. I began contemplating settling down somewhere in Germany.

By the time the Olympics started in Los Angeles, John had returned to the States, and my wife came to stay with me in a German hotel. We watched the Olympic track-and-field events from our hotel room, and I was disheartened, realizing how far I had sunk in just a few months' time. Though I should have been in my running prime, due to the wear my alcoholism had taken on my body, not to mention the bridges I had necessarily burned in the running world, I felt my chances to return to elite form were waning, if not past. Still, I was also hopeful of establishing a stable life for my family and me and would happily give up track and field all together if I could somehow build a strong foundation for our future.

By this time, the hostilities I suffered in Kenya led me to believe that it would be impossible to live a peaceful and prosperous life there. Though I tried to convince my wife that the best prospects for our future would be outside Kenya and that we should consider buying a house and settling down in Germany, she felt too many connections to the culture of our homeland. I sympathized with her need to remain in the country where she was raised and had always lived, and so, with an ominous feeling that I refrained from articulating to my wife, we returned to Molo.

Chapter XXI
Return to the United States

Late 1984 through the spring of 1986 was a blur to me. Upon returning to Kenya, my depression worsened. The threats, both direct and implicit, over my farmland continued. I didn't feel safe. By December of 1984, I felt my family and I were in danger living in Molo, and so we moved to a humble house in Nairobi. In Nairobi, to assuage my anxieties, I would often drink all day, feeling incapable of leaving the couch. At times, I would leave my family for one or two months and head to my home village of Kiptaragon and drink *chang'aa* and hang out with vagrant alcoholics until I passed out in doorways or on the streets. When I was away, my wife would tell me of the threatening calls she had received from my neighbor and others about my farmland.

In February of 1986, after I had finished last in the national cross-country championships, a sympathetic KAAA official, Charles Mukora, found me depressed and binge drinking in the Midland Hotel in Nakuru.

"I think someone twisted your arm from 1982 through 1984. You should consider heading back to the United States to get well," he told me.

As simple as his words were, they served as a resounding wake-up call to me. I called Abraham Hussein, who bought me a ticket to the United States, and, by May 1986, I was living in Albuquerque, New Mexico, resuming my training with Hussein and other Kenyan runners who had gravitated to the high desert of Albuquerque to train.

By July of 1986, though still out of shape and overweight, I felt ready to compete in small local meets. I competed in such a race in New Jersey, where I met John DeHart, an athletic trainer who owned state-of-the-art workout facilities. DeHart convinced me to stay in New Jersey and train under his supervision, promising that he could help me shed my extra pounds and get me back into peak physical shape in no time. I agreed, and soon I had trimmed a great deal of fat from my physique, as well as considerable seconds off my times in local meets.

Returning to running had tempered my drinking. Still, I would fluctuate from dedicating myself almost exclusively to my training one week to drinking heavily the next. The amount I drank in a given week depended largely on my emotional well-being. Fortunately, my mental state was enhanced with every improvement in my running. Soon, I was winning local races, making $500 or so for every victory and slowly returning to a vague semblance of the form I had known only four years previously. Still, I was a long cry from competing at an elite level, and, though improvements in my running had dramatically lifted my spirits, I still had an overriding uneasiness, which manifested itself in an intense fear of failing in upcoming races.

Chapter XXII
A Case of Mistaken Identity

On a bitterly cold November morning in 1986, I walked into a bank in Hackensack, New Jersey to open an account in which I intended to deposit the money I won in a recent marathon. I had told my family in Kenya just a few hours previously that I would wire money to them just as soon as I opened an account. Inside the bank, a teller told me that opening an account would require a $25 administrative fee. I replied that I only had $30 on me, and so first I wanted to go get some breakfast since I was ravenously hungry from my morning run. If I had enough money left after breakfast, I planned on returning directly to the bank. If, however, my breakfast cost more than five dollars, I would have to first head to my apartment in order to get more cash.

Unfortunately, I never had a chance to get breakfast that morning. As I was walking out of the bank, five policemen—two in uniform and three in plainclothes—surrounded and started interrogating me. One asked for my identification and my name. I gave him my ID and said, "Henry Rono." One of the policemen shot me a sly look. "Are you sure you're Henry Rono?" he asked. Apparently, I'd never noticed that the last name on my ID was misspelled "Rond," so the officers immediately suspected that I was using a false identity.

Just then, the teller handed the policemen a mug shot of a man who looked nothing like me except that he was Black and asked if I knew him. I later learned that the person in the photo was suspected of robbing a number of banks in the area. When I told them that I didn't know the person, they asked again as if it to imply that they were certain that the photo was of me. The officers then asked me where I lived, and I told them that I lived two blocks away. I took them to my apartment and, as we approached the front door, they asked me for my key. Before we entered into my apartment, they handcuffed me and asked to see my room. After finding nothing incriminating in my room, we proceeded to the living room and then to the kitchen, where the policemen became interested in a cassette player on the dining room table. In the player was a sports motivational tape that my trainer John DeHart had given me and that I had been listening to. They pushed play, and the voice through the speaker lectured on about sports psychology. After the officers finished listening to the tape, they took me to a police car, where I sat in the back with the two uniformed policemen in the front. Following us to the police station in an unmarked car were the three plainclothesmen and the bank teller, who was to serve as a witness. As we neared the police station, I looked out the rear window at the unmarked car behind us, where the teller waved at me with a smirk on her face, as if to say, "Gotcha!"

At the precinct, I told my interrogators I was not a thief, but a runner. When they asked me for the name of my coach, I told them his name was John DeHart and that he was a local trainer. Unfortunately, when the detectives called DeHart, he wouldn't vouch for me. As a result, I was taken to a jail cell. After a few minutes, a policeman came to my cell and asked if I wanted to speak with my coach, and I told him yes. On the phone, DeHart sounded more like one of the cops than one of my friends. He asked me, "Do you know why you're there?" When I told him no, he said that it was because of my bank robbing. He told me that I had finally been apprehended for the six bank robberies I had committed throughout New Jersey. He and the police speculated that I actually would run to the banks to rob them or that it was somehow a part of my training regimen. I had known DeHart for only a few months, and, apparently in that time, he had not gotten to know me well enough to realize that it was not in my character to rob banks.

Once I was booked, I underwent the exhaustive medical exams required for prison admission. One of the doctors recognized me and said, "I saw you just a few days ago at the New York City Marathon. You're in the wrong place." After the exams, I put on my prison uniform, and then a guard gave me a mattress and a blanket and walked me to a very crowded dormitory, where he stopped me in front of a double bunk bed and said, "You are going to sleep here." As I sat in the cell, I screamed to one of the guards, "I'm hungry—I have to eat! You put me here, and I didn't do anything. I will sue for a million dollars." He told me to let him know when I got that million dollars.

As I walked toward my bed, a few Black inmates welcomed me. I told them I was hungry, and one of the inmates handed me two bags of cereal, a carton of milk, and a packet of sugar. I took a deep breath and felt relieved. After I ate my belated breakfast, I lay down and tried to sleep. Before I did, the inmate who gave me the cereal and was now laying in the bunk below me said, "Guess what? You have to pay for the cereal." I told him I didn't have money, though I left $30 at the main office. He replied, "Okay, that should be enough," and told me to have the guard put the money in his account. I told him I would. The dormitory hall I was in was exclusively for Black prisoners. I later learned there were halls devoted exclusively to Latinos and still others for Whites.

I didn't sleep that night. At 4:00 AM, guards arrived to wake the prisoners in my dormitory for breakfast. At breakfast, I encountered a football-field-sized cafeteria packed full of thousands of inmates, most of whom appeared to be Black or Latino. Entering the bustling cafeteria, I thought to myself that there seemed to be more people in prison in New Jersey than there were people living free.

After breakfast, I returned to my bunk bed. As I was sitting there, the guy who sold me cereal the night before kept approaching me and asking random questions, all the while flashing me the centerfold of a pornographic magazine. Another inmate approached me and said that he had seen me on TV and also in *Sports Illustrated*. "You used to be a famous runner, didn't you?" he asked.

Before long, all the inmates in my bunk seemed to know about my celebrity, and a crowd began to gather around me. I told the inmates that I felt like running, though what I really felt like was getting away from all the scrutiny. I went around the dormitory, which was about 75 yards long, and cleared a path between the bunk beds. Then I began running between the bunks at a slow pace since my body was stiff from my lack of sleep. After a few laps, my muscles warmed up and soon I was running at a pretty fair clip.

The inmates watched me and stood along my path cheering and clapping their hands. As I zoomed past them, I could hear some of them saying, "I've seen him on TV." I started feeling much more relaxed as the intimidation I felt when surrounded by the crowd of inmates dissipated. I was simply enjoying my running, and the place no longer seemed to matter—this dormitory might as well have been the track at WSU or the woods outside of Eugene—until the guard yelled out to me, "If you try to escape, I will shoot you." When the inmates heard this they yelled back at him, "No, he's just an Olympic runner doing his workout!" I ran for a good 80 to 90 minutes and felt quite relieved. Later that day, I did a longer run, probably 10 miles or so, and once again felt as though I was outside doing my usual workout.

    After my second run, I took a shower and returned to my bunk. That's when I noticed my running shoes were gone. I asked around, and the same guy who sold me cereal told me he knew someone who knew someone else who could get my shoes back, but it would cost me. "You'll be needing them for your next workout, won't you?" he prodded. Then he told me 50 bucks would get them back. "Put the money in my account, and I'll get you your shoes back," he told me. When I told him that the only money I had was the $30 I paid him for cereal, he asked, "Could you call a friend to loan you the money to put into my account?"

I made a number of calls to friends and acquaintances before I was able to convince my buddy Andrew to transfer the money for me. "Who is this guy selling you things in prison and asking you for money to buy back your own shoes?" Andrew asked me. After he got off of the phone with me, Andrew called the prison's main office to ask why I was not only in prison, but being harassed and robbed by inmates. "Henry is a celebrity and a legend and he is not supposed to be there," Andrew told the prison administrators. Soon after Andrew got off the phone with the prison administrators, a prison guard approached me and told me to pick up my mattress and blanket. I followed him back to the main office, where I exited the lobby and got into a car that took me to a prison for celebrities and high-profile inmates where I would have not only my own room, but a number of amenities and even luxuries not afforded inmates in normal prisons.

At the celebrity prison, they brought food directly to my cell, which was actually quite a comfortable room, replete with a TV, personal shower, and plenty of reading material. The person in the cell adjacent to mine was pleasant and articulate, and we had a number of good conversations during my time there. The only drawback about the celebrity prison was that there was no space to run in. Still, I carried on with my training, lifting my knees up and down in place, starting slowly and building to a high speed until I finished my stationary run one hour and 15 minutes later.

Near the end of my first day in the celebrity jail, I got a call from a woman in the Kenyan Embassy who asked about the conditions in the prisons. In addition to expressing her surprise at learning that I was able to keep up my training routine in my cell, she told me that my lawyer and the authorities should have everything sorted out by Monday. After I got off the phone with the woman from the Kenyan embassy, my lawyer, Merrill Rubin, introduced himself and said that he was sent by the agent to come and speak with me. He told me my court date would be Monday and that he thought he would be able to prove my innocence.

In the celebrity prison, a number of high-profile lawyers went around soliciting inmates. One of these lawyers came to my cell and asked if I was Henry Rono. When I answered yes, he told me he wasn't soliciting me to be his client, but rather that he just wanted to shake my hand since I was his hero.

On Monday, I was escorted with handcuffs and shackles on my legs to the courtroom by five armed policemen and my lawyer. It was all but impossible to walk with shackles on, and I had to resort to a sort of mix between stepping, shuffling, and jumping in order to keep up with my escorts. In the courtroom, my judge told me, "You have been accused of robbing four banks in different counties in the state of New Jersey." My day in court lasted 18 hours, and, by the time I was proven innocent and released, it was after midnight. As I was saying thank you and goodbye to my lawyer, he told me, "We've learned something about the justice system in this state. The prisons are inherently racist, and, if you were not famous, they could have locked you up for life like they do with so many innocent prisoners."

At the end of all these court proceedings, the banks apologized and tried to make an out-of-court settlement worth $50,000. Rubin convinced me not to accept the settlement, saying, "We'll sue the bank for ten million!" The lawsuit took two years to settle, and we won $75,000, of which—after Rubin took his share of $35, 000—I ended up seeing 40 grand.

After my six days of wrongful imprisonment in New Jersey, I checked myself into a rehabilitation center in Philadelphia. I stayed there 14 days until I felt I could handle my life without a counselor's help. I walked out of that program on my own strength and moved to Boston, where an old friend from England invited me to live with him until I found my own apartment. In Boston, I began drinking again after workouts, going to the bar around 2:00 PM and staying until 10:00 PM, when I felt ready to pass out and so returned to my apartment to get some sleep. Sometimes, I found that mixing different types of alcohol made my sleep restless. One particular night, I woke up at 2:00 AM and couldn't fall back asleep. I got dressed and went out, thinking maybe I might find one of the bars still open.

When I went out, I found that all the bars were closed. As I was walking back to my apartment, I came across a group of Mexicans who were having a small street party. I asked if they could spare a bottle of beer. They said yes, and I thanked them. It was a very cold winter night, and I had on an overcoat. I later wondered whether this made the Mexicans suspect I was a detective or someone else sinister. I quickly finished the beer and asked for more. A couple of Mexicans asked me to follow them next door where they said they would ask for more beer for me. Suddenly, they jumped me, and I was left lying on the ground bleeding from my forehead. Unable to walk, I crawled and drug myself back to my apartment. By the time my roommate found me the next morning, I was shaking and my teeth were chattering. I told my roommate that I didn't want the media to know about the incident. Still, he insisted on rushing me to a local hospital, where I found my rib cage was broken close to my heart. One of the doctors told me that my ribs could easily have punctured my heart and I could have died.

In those days, I was living day to day and even minute to minute. It was a critical point in my life. Giving up alcohol seemed impossible to me. In order to even consider doing so, I first had to have an encounter with death. After my beating, I admitted myself to a rehabilitation center in New York. In the coming years, I would be in and out of seven rehabilitation programs before I was even able to comprehend the scope and roots of my addiction.

Chapter XXIII
The Return of Cooper and Mibey

With the 1988 Seoul Summer Olympics on the horizon, two bad memories from years past returned. Gordon Cooper once again had James Mibey approach me—this time with an offer to sponsor my training for the Olympics. I was a wayward soul during this time of my life, drinking heavily, and, while I don't remember agreeing to Cooper's proposition, I do recall feeling helpless to deny it. I remembered what a hell Cooper could make of my life whenever I refused his influence, and the truth is I was living like a vagrant in those days, drifting from town to town, with my alcoholism making me vulnerable to others' devices for me.

While Mibey wanted Cooper to set up training camp for me near Los Angeles, where he could indulge in the fast-paced

California nightlife, Cooper had a more remote location in mind, figuring that putting Mibey and me in a non-urban area, where we would be unable to understand the language, would curb my drinking and Mibey's fraternizing to allow me to focus solely on training. Before long, Cooper shipped Mibey and me off to a remote Mexican island off the coast of Tijuana that usually only served as a swanky fishing destination for the wealthy. As he prepared to leave us at our beach hotel, Cooper's parting words to me were, "Stay focused: this is an ideal training spot for you." Then he turned to Mibey, "Make sure he doesn't drink."

While Cooper may have been right to think that the isolated island was an ideal training locale, I was not in the right mind-set to embrace a serious training regimen. My past experience living with Mibey left me with distaste for him and being forced to associate solely with him for an extended period of time only fueled my desire to drink while extinguishing all my remaining ambition to train. After just a few weeks on the island, I was drinking myself into a comatose state each evening to cope with having to interact with Mibey, which only drew me deeper into the depression I only became aware of during the last weeks of my stay on the island when I began corresponding with a sports psychologist at Oregon State University, who sent me volumes of psychology textbooks and journals for me to read during my stay in Mexico.

During my time on the island, I displayed all the classic symptoms of depression. I became increasingly dependent on alcohol to help me cope with my emotional stress, and I found it impossible to focus on my training and equally impossible to have a non-confrontational relationship with Mibey. There were times when Mibey and I got into such heated arguments that I came close to beating him up. One night after an especially volatile row over my not training, I stayed up drinking while Mibey retired to his room and fell asleep. In the very earliest hours of the morning, I burst into his room yelling, "You want me to train? Then let's go train." He looked at me with both fear and exhaustion in his eyes, staring at me as if I were mad. I pulled him out of bed and told him, "Let's go train. You always want me to go train. Then get up—let's go!"

I ran all along the beach for hours through the dark that morning, demanding Mibey to keep up despite his tiredness and drunkenness. After it looked like Mibey was about to expire behind me, I ran back to our hotel. After this incident, Mibey thought I was truly crazy and never again directly confronted me about my excessive drinking or lack of training. From then on, he left me to my own devices, which consisted primarily of pouring over my psychology texts.

Cooper must have paid the hotel manager to keep watch over Mibey and me since he showed up the day after our big blowout and threatened Mibey for not keeping me on track with my training and for letting me drink. Mibey looked like he was about to break into tears. Once Cooper had left, though, nothing changed, and, after a few weeks, Mibey and I had another major blowout that made the hotel manager call Cooper again. Cooper visited Mibey and me three times during our six-week stay in Mexico, and, after the third visit, it must have been apparent to him that trying to get me to sober up and get in shape for the Seoul Olympics was hopeless. I was a depressed alcoholic, and Cooper must have realized I was beyond help at this point—or, rather, he must have realized that the type of rehabilitation my condition required would take longer than the half-year remaining before the Olympics were to begin.

In February of 1988, Cooper bought Mibey and me a boat ride back to the mainland. When we arrived in Tijuana, Cooper picked us up in his car, and we rode in silence for a long while before we reached the border. Before Cooper let us out of the car, he turned to me and in a kind tone said, "Henry, I want you to know that I only wanted what was best for you. I don't want you to think that I ever intended to harm you. Now I want you to take care of yourself." Cooper then asked me what I thought I would do with myself now, and I told him I just wanted to make a plain and simple living with my hands. Then Cooper turned to Mibey, his brow furrowed and his voice whittled down to a point, saying, "I could have shot you and dumped you in the desert with the gun at your side, and, in the unlikely occasion that the *federales* would have contacted the FBI, I could have told them you must have killed yourself out of jealousy for Henry Rono." Cooper paused, rubbed his knuckles against his scalp, and then glanced at me before fixing his glare on Mibey once more, "You've done the same thing to Henry that you did to him before the '84 Olympics." Then he told us to get out of the car.

Before I crossed the border, Mibey and I sat down for beers at a Tijuana tavern. Mibey started to cry, saying that he had no passport and would never be able to cross and that it was all my fault that he would likely be left to die in Mexico. After my beer, I approached the border, where five Mexican border patrol officials approached me. I showed them my passport and, because Cooper had provided me with a nice suit for my return to the States, the patrol officers treated me with dignity and respect. I later heard that Mibey was arrested at the border and spent a good deal of time in a Mexican prison.

Chapter XXIV
New Beginnings, But No Resolution

When I was back on the American side of the border, I looked for a pay phone and decided to call John Chaplin, who pretended he didn't know me and then hung up. Fortunately, Reed Harvey—an American whom I had befriended when I was living in New Jersey in 1986 and who, years later, would visit my family in Kenya for me and eventually become a humanitarian aid worker throughout Africa—came looking for me and took me to New York, where I began trying to regain my motivation for training. However, that summer, as I awaited the settlement from my New Jersey court case, I realized that what would be my last realistic chance at an Olympic games had passed, and soon my depression and drinking worsened, making it impossible for me to train effectively or take running seriously. By August, I was admitted into a rehabilitation center in Rochester, New York.

I was in the rehab center while the Seoul Olympics were underway, and one day a counselor told me, "Your brother Peter Rono is going to win a gold medal in the 1,500 meters." The counselors put me in a special room by myself where I watched all the track-and-field events. Under head coach Mike Kosgei, the 1988 games proved to be the most successful Olympics in Kenyan history as Kenyan runners won a variety of events, from the 800 meters to the marathon. Watching the Olympics brought a great deal of clarity to my mind, and, on that very day, I accepted that alcohol was my enemy and realized if I could stop my drinking, I still had a prayer at a good life.

In the spring of 1989, I returned to Eugene and enrolled in classes in sports psychology at the University of Oregon. Unfortunately, I could not attend the classes since I was broke and had been denied financial assistance. I looked for a job to help me pay for classes, but could find none. I even approached my old friends at the Nike headquarters at Beaverton and told them I would be willing to do anything, even clean their floors, if they would provide me with a minimum-wage salary. They brusquely turned me down.

My difficulties in finding work were amplified by my immigration status in the United States. My green card had been stalled at the U.S. Immigration and Naturalization Office for years. I heard about a chicken soup factory in Oregon that welcomed illegal workers in order to increase their profits with cheap labor. I applied and was hired in the spring of 1989. My first day on the job, I noticed my co-workers were staring at me. In the afternoon, the boss asked me to follow him to the office. "Does the news media follow you around?" the boss asked me, saying that I was on TV the previous night. He handed me $40 and told me never to show my face at his factory again. My life had reached a new low point. I was unemployed, broke, and without a place to stay, so I checked into a local rescue mission.

I moved to Portland in the spring of 1990 where I was introduced to the pastor of New Beginnings Church, who used to run drugs between Columbia and the United States before becoming a born-again Christian. The rehabilitation program at New Beginnings was rigorous, which appealed to the penchant for discipline I inherited from my military training in the Kenyan Army. The counselors at New Beginnings told me to forget my running routine and instead focus on training my spirit. Instead of getting up and running at 5:00 AM, I got up to meditate and then read the Bible. I could read the Bible and feel as though the Scriptures were specifically addressing me. I would meditate or sing hymns for hours at a time and feel spiritually and emotionally reinvigorated.

While in New Beginnings program, Mike Boit's wife arrived in Portland to see me. She said her husband, who was now the Kenyan Commissioner of Sports, sent her to convince me to return to Kenya. Mrs. Boit asked me about my rehabilitation program, questioning whether it was helpful to my recovery. I told her it had worked amazingly well and that I felt more stable and happy than I could ever remember feeling. Instead of accepting my comments at face value, she became hostile, disputing that faith could ever cure alcoholism. After our short argument over this issue passed, she told me the reason she came was to offer me a job that the Kenyan government had waiting for me. I responded by matter-of-factly telling her that I had no intention of ever returning to Kenya.

Finally, as a desperate last resort to persuade me, she blurted out, "Your wife is seeing another man!" I told her that that sounded just like the same old manipulative lies I was accustomed to from Mike Boit. Sadly, once he assumed office, Boit became just another exploitative appendage of the KAAA. Even more upsetting is that he became most exploitative of those runners who, like him, were Nandi. Still, even though I wasn't willing to submit to his desires for me, Boit continued to seek my approval for the job he was doing as commissioner. Once, as if to impress me, he assured me he was in the process of creating a program to encourage athletic scholarships to colleges in Kenya to slow the exodus of Kenyan runners to American universities. He told me this 13 years ago, and I am still waiting for it.

Chapter XXV
One Last Long Shot at the Olympics

In August 1990, I moved from Portland to Albuquerque to get back into competitive running shape and attempt the professional comeback I felt ready for after my intensive spiritual healing. While running in the Duke City Marathon, I bumped into another Kenyan runner, Sammy Sitonik. Sitonik made several attempts to pass me, but I was stubborn and increased my pace to compensate for his surges. Realizing I wasn't going to allow him to pass me, he said, "Let's run and finish together. Then we can talk about a training plan after the race." Realizing that neither of us was in contention to win the race, I agreed. Together, we accelerated toward the finish line, both finishing the 21 kilometers in 74 minutes.

After the race, we decided to train together for the 1992 Olympics, and Sitonik invited me to stay with him and his family in Las Vegas, Nevada while we trained. Training in the desert hills of Nevada, we improved our marathon times by 10 minutes in only two weeks. Sitonik was shocked by our rapid improvement, as was his boss at the company he worked for, who saw our progress as justification for his generous sponsorship of our training. I placed second in a Las Vegas half-marathon, with Sitonik finishing fourth, and soon the press was buzzing about yet another Henry Rono comeback. I began receiving phone calls from fans who simply wanted to encourage me on my comeback. A few weeks later, I won a half-marathon in Austin, Texas, and my comeback was now making international sports news as it became apparent to the world that, after being denied the chance to compete in two Olympics by the Kenyan government and then squandering two other chances at the Olympics because of depression and alcoholism, my eyes were set firmly on the improbable goal of reaching the 1992 Barcelona Olympics at the age of 40.

Unfortunately, just as my comeback seemed most promising, the media attention became a major source of stress and anxiety for me. Ever since 1986, when I returned to America to resume my training, I had been marred by a fear of failure. And, ironically, the more attention and accolades I received for my running, the more I came to doubt my abilities. Soon John Chaplin was criticizing me in the press, and I felt distracted and nervous. Before I knew it, I was drinking heavily again to deal with my fear and anxiety. My drinking led to a falling out with Sitonik and, realizing I was settling back into my usual crisis mode, I checked myself into a rescue mission in Las Vegas for a week before returning to New Mexico.

In Albuquerque, I resumed training with a number of my countrymen, including marathoners Douglas Wakihuri and Abraham Hussein, who were preparing for the Barcelona Olympics by running in Albuquerque's thin high-desert air. As a middle-distance runner, my training for the marathon was a bit crude and unconventional. Still, I held fast to my hopes to qualify for the marathon in the upcoming Olympics.

I soon returned to running competitively, participating in small races across the country. In May of 1991, I ran the Pittsburgh Marathon, and, though I didn't place in the money bracket, I claimed a $2,000 appearance fee for the event, which was a lot of money for me as I was basically living hand-to-mouth at the time. The money from the Pittsburgh Marathon helped keep me afloat for a few months.

Just as the money I earned in the Pittsburgh Marathon was running out, I came under siege from meet directors about various financial debts they said I owed them. As a result of my financial problems, I became depressed and yet again returned to drinking. However, I soon realized that I was returning to the same vicious cycle, and so I checked myself into a 30-day program at a California treatment center.

After my month in treatment, I decided to stay in California and train in low altitude. I found a coaching job at Huntington Beach High School. That year, though I was turning 40, being able to train with prep runners made me feel younger than I had felt in many years. I showed these high school runners a variety of my training techniques, including the intensive hill climbing routine I had practiced in Gilgil. My pupils embraced my techniques, and their new training routines resulted in a drastic overall improvement for the Huntington Beach High track squad that spring.

Chapter XXVI
Destruction at Molo Farm

On April 24, 1992, while I was coaching in California, I received a devastating telephone call from my wife in Kenya. She said an unknown gang had raided our Molo farm, setting fire to all that would burn, stealing all of our livestock, including 70 heads of cattle, and killing two of my workers. Still, my wife considered herself lucky that day since, had she been on the Molo farm, she would likely also have been killed. I couldn't help but suspect my neighbor Nge'ny, who continually had the nerve to insist my wife and I sell him our land.

I figured that Nge'ny must have thought that the destruction would frighten my wife and me enough to convince us to give up the farm. When Nge'ny's harassment continued after the destruction of our farm, my wife contacted local authorities and told them about the series of intimidating calls she and I had received from Nge'ny ever since we purchased the farm a decade earlier and how our fears grew with each contact from Nge'ny until the raid on our farm. The government's response to our allegations was swift, but involved no true punishment for Nge'ny, who was transferred from his position as the Molo district's postmaster to another district, where he was to hold a similar government office and was compensated for the inconvenience of his transfer with a plot of land of comparable worth to the one he owned in Molo.

In 1992, we abandoned the Molo farm since, after the crops and buildings were burned and our livestock pillaged, it was no longer economically viable to try and return the farm to an operable condition. It was a big financial hit on my family as the rich farmland of Molo had produced between $15,000 and $20,000 of yearly income for us. Growing ever more desperate for money, in 1994, Jennifer and I considered trying to reconstruct the farm until another threat came from a neighbor, who told us, "I don't think you would be safe there." Though Nge'ny had moved away from his farm in Molo, he still owned and operated the property, and his employees had torn down the barbed wire fence that separated his property from mine to use my land as a pasture for his cattle.

With the declaration of wealth policy initiated by Kenya's current president, Mwai Kibaki, I remain cautiously optimistic about my prospects of renovating my land in Molo and once again using the land as a primary source of income someday. Still, the last time I was in Molo Town, which was over a dozen years ago, I came across one of the government potato-farm surveyors inspecting the region's farmland. I mentioned that I had long ago applied for the title deed for my land, but had still not received it. He told me that since my land had already been surveyed and paid, I should receive it by 1994. I have still yet to receive the title to my Molo land, which must be cleared before I could even consider returning my farm to an operable condition.

Chapter XXVII
The Salt Lake City Salvation Army Blues

In 1992, I was living in a halfway house in Salt Lake City when a Salvation Army representative came looking to hire a worker to collect donations for their annual holiday fundraiser. The representative explained that for five dollars an hour, my job would be to stand outside a department store beside a red donation bucket while ringing a small silver bell for Christmas shoppers. I thought of how cold it would be standing outside for hours at a time exposed to the frigid winds blowing off the Great Salt Lake. But I needed to make money in order to leave the halfway house and I couldn't afford to turn down any job at that point in my life.

After my first week on the job, the Salvation Army representative was pleased to tell me that I was doing a good job of shaking my little bell as my station was collecting money at a rate well above average. One day, when I was on my fifteen-minute break, I decided to get out of the cold and go into the department store I'd been standing in front of. A heavy wool sweater and a thick pair of pants caught my eye, and I told myself, "These would be a well-deserved Christmas present to yourself, Henry. They'll help you stay warm in the sub-freezing Salt Lake temperatures."

The sweater and pants were affordable, but after I received my first Salvation Army check, I realized that I couldn't spare that much money on clothes. Then I said to myself, "Wait, I know how I can get the money." When people approached the bucket with a dollar bill, I reached out my hand to take the money from them instead of letting them place their money in the bucket themselves; I then went through the motion of placing the bill in the slot, but what I really did is tuck the bill deep in my hand, clamping it against my palm with my thumb; then I casually moved my hand to my jacket pocket.

I pocketed a dollar here and then another there and told myself that it was okay to take a few more dollars until I was able to afford the sweater and pants. However, it did not take long for the Salvation Army representative to realize that my station's collections dipped drastically, and soon she moved me to a station at another mall where she could keep an eye on me through security cameras set up in the parking lots and on the facades of the store entrances. Unaware of the surveillance, I pocketed my first few dollars, and soon after the Salvation Army representative approached me. I expected the worst, thinking that she would fire me on the spot and maybe even contact the authorities. However, she was not harsh or confrontational when she spoke to me and she simply asked me in a stern but polite tone to please stop keeping the money in my pocket and to let the donors put their bills in the bucket themselves. Then, in a voice more sad than upset, she said, "This money is for men like you, Henry, who are homeless or having a hard time making it." I put my head down in shame and nodded. Maybe it was because I didn't deny pocketing the money, or maybe she could tell from my shameful expression that I was not usually a deceitful person, but for whatever reason, she was pleasant and sympathetic to me, and for this I owe her my gratitude. From the moment the Salvation Army representative apprehended me, I never pocketed another dollar, and, to this day, I am remorseful for the money I stole—which was money I kept from my fellow homeless brothers.

Chapter XXVIII
The Twelfth Step

One of the few bright spots during what was an otherwise dismal span of years for me in the early 1990s came in 1993, when I lived in Shiprock, New Mexico and worked as an assistant track coach at Navajo Community College (NCC). While there, I developed a running regimen that I called the "Shiprock Project," which helped lead NCC to its first National Small College Championship that year. Unfortunately, NCC ran out of funding for the Shiprock Project after one year, which left me looking for employment elsewhere.

In June of 1994, I visited my cousin in Washington, DC, where he worked as a driver for the Kenyan Embassy. While staying with my cousin, I spoke openly to him of my ongoing struggle with alcoholism and how the spiritual regimen emphasized by New Beginnings Church had helped me remain sober. My cousin, who was a habitual drinker if not an alcoholic, became testy with my candor about the negative effects that alcohol had had on my life.

Later that week, without first getting my approval, my cousin arranged for me to attend an athletic banquet as a speaker and guest of honor. I told my cousin that I didn't feel like attending the event, much less speaking at it, especially after he had treated me with such hostility earlier in the week. After the banquet, the media came to the post-banquet reception held at my cousin's house and wanted to know why I hadn't accepted my guest of honor invitation. Since I felt uneasy and awkward about missing the banquet and because I felt a great deal of social anxiety about entertaining the guests who arrived early to my cousin's reception, I began drinking. After the party, now drunk and belligerent, I got into a terrible argument with my cousin. The next morning, he kicked me out of his house. Suddenly, I was homeless again, and so I sought shelter at the Salvation Army, where I stayed for four months while undergoing a 12-step program for alcoholism.

At the Salvation Army, I participated in another of their work programs for the homeless, which paid me a dollar a day. By the end of the week, I used my seven dollars to pay for telephone calls to my family and stamps. During this time, a local minister, Pastor Yego, and his family offered me a great deal of support and encouragement, which helped me to regain enough physical and emotional strength to help me overcome my alcoholism in a comprehensive and lasting way. After the four months receiving treatment in DC, I felt ready to head out on my own, and so I moved back to a region I was familiar with, the Pacific Northwest, where I settled in Portland, Oregon.

In early 1995, when I arrived in Portland, I contacted everyone from old friends in the area to Nike representatives and even Coach Chaplin, seeking employment. Every time I contacted one of my old acquaintances or visited their offices, I was given the runaround and told to come back another time. Eventually, I decided to look for menial jobs. First, I got a job as a used car salesmen. The manager of the dealership figured I was at least a marginal regional celebrity and that perhaps my star power, however much it might have dimmed in the last decade, might still attract customers. However, I was too sensitive to customers' needs and problems, not to mention too honest, to be a good car salesman.

For instance, one time an eighteen-year-old girl who had just graduated from high school came into the manager's office crying. One of the other salesmen had sold her a lemon with a nice paint job for the price of a gently used and well-maintained vehicle. She drove it home and the car broke down on the way. I quit immediately once I realized the deceit my job would require.

I found another job a few weeks later working as a parking lot attendant. I was parking cars underneath high buildings in a garage and washing them before their owners returned. Soon the media had got word of my working a menial job and proceeded to play up the cliché story of the once-heroic athlete who came upon hard times. When Oregonian sports columnist Steve Duin found me, he asked, "How come you are here and your rival Salazar practically owns Nike? Did you ask them for a job?" I told him that I approached Nike for any job, even if it meant cleaning their floors, but they turned me down. Still, I told him that I was content with my current job, which paid me well enough to get by and allowed me to work on my training log in my downtime. In fact, I was the happiest I had been in quite a long while as I enjoyed the rigor of my daily schedule, and I went straight from working a full-time job during the day to training for master's division races in the evening. Though my times in these races were often very slow, running had returned to being what it once was for me: a joyful and meditative activity.

After Duin's story was published, it hit the wires and soon spin-off stories were being published in international sports pages. In Kenya, the sports officials were embarrassed to have me get this exposure, which made it seem as though they had turned their back on me, which, of course, they had. After the stories of my alcoholism and financial demise hit international papers, KAAA officials contacted my family as if they hadn't known of, or, for that matter played an integral part in, my struggles and strife all these years.

Once an American sportswriter broke the story of my life, both local and international journalists began to hound me. I despised the attention and just wanted to begin a new life of anonymity, working an honorable job and fitting into society just like everyone else. At this point, I decided to move back to Albuquerque, where the local media would not be as interested in my story since I had no collegiate or professional ties to the area and because Albuquerque is not the track-and-field hotbed that most cities in the Pacific Northwest are.

I returned to Albuquerque in 1996, relying on a variety of menial jobs to help me stay financially afloat. However, for once in my life I had a long-term goal: I wanted to become a high school special education teacher, and I began pursuing my teaching certification and applying for positions in Albuquerque and surrounding school districts. When I was growing up, my curiosity and articulateness, as well as my inherent desire to help my peers and explain things to them, made my mother believe I would someday become a teacher. This was still my dream while attending WSU. However, somewhere along the way, as I pursued my running career and struggled with my problems with the KAAA, as well as with Chaplin, various agents, meet directors, and my neighbor in Molo, I lost sight of my dream. Now with the beginning of a new millennium and having been sober for many years, I felt ready to return to the pursuit of my teaching dream.

By the fall of 1996, along with working as a skycap at Albuquerque International Airport part time and taking six hours of classes at UNM to earn my teacher's license, I began substitute teaching for Albuquerque Public Schools (APS). Soon I became a full-time substitute at Albuquerque's Valley High School (VHS).

In the late summer of 1997, I accepted an offer from Chris Jaramillo, the head cross-country and track coach at VHS, to serve as his assistant coach and help resuscitate his school's struggling running programs. The VHS cross-country squad, which had been a pushover in the years before my arrival, made rapid improvements after adopting my training regimen, and many of their runners excelled in that year's state championships. The Albuquerque papers and broadcast media soon picked up on the feel-good story of a world-record breaker who had come out of the woodwork to help a struggling high school program. Jaramillo was a big, gregarious man with a good heart who hadn't received the credit he deserved for slaving over a high-school running program with very little tradition. Jaramillo was not accustomed to his program receiving so much attention, so he relished every time his name appeared in the papers or his name on TV.

While I was volunteering at Valley High School, I had been approached by Shawn Hellebuyck, an agent living in Albuquerque who had a reputation for taking advantage of her clients, especially runners who were unaware of their rights because of their unfamiliarity with American culture, their lack of education, or their inability to communicate well in English. I first learned of Hellebuyck's exploitative tactics when I moved to Albuquerque in 1996. At that time, a number of young Kenyan runners training in Albuquerque sought me out for advice. Many of these runners were having trouble with their agent, whom they said was not depositing their winnings or appearance fees in their accounts and then blaming this on meet directors. I later learned this agent was Hellebuyck.

The most blatant instance of Hellebuyck's corruption involved Benson Masya, the Kenyan runner who reminded so many track aficionados of me. Not only was he a prodigiously talented runner, he was also a person who, like me, reacted to the stress of the exploitation he suffered by turning to drink. Hellebuyck took advantage of Masya's alcoholism just as many coaches and agents had taken advantage of my addiction. Knowing that Masya's drunkenness fogged his memory and made him susceptible to exploitation, Hellebuyck blatantly stole from him. Once, when he returned from a meet in Mexico, Masya asked why his $20,000 winnings had not been deposited into his bank account. Hellebuyck, who handled Masya's accounts and received his paychecks, claimed to not have received the payment from the meet director in Mexico and so sent Masya on a wild goose hunt through Mexico to try and track down the meet director. When he finally did, the meet director showed him a receipt for the $20,000 with Hellebuyck's signature on it.

Of course, Hellebuyck's manipulation of Masya was just one of her countless exploitations of foreign athletes. However, not all of her corrupt dealings with athletes went without consequence. I heard a funny story of a time when Hellebuyck was busy recruiting athletes during the New York City Marathon. As she was waiting for an elevator at her swanky hotel, a Kenyan athlete whom she had cheated out of $1,000 spotted her and then proceeded to jump on her back, grab her by the neck, and tell her he wasn't going to let go until she forked over the money she had stolen from him. She tossed off a check to him that very moment to literally get him off her back!

The more I learned about Hellebuyck's exploitative nature, the more it made me want to serve as a mentor and advocate for these runners who had come under her influence. Many years of being exploited by meet directors, coaches, agents, and athletic officials made me sympathize with the corruption they were encountering.

I often tried to connect these exploited runners with officials and professionals whom I knew to be fair. Hellebuyck felt threatened by what she perceived to be my meddling in *her* runners' careers and forbade them from associating with me.

At one point, she even threatened to call the police if I continued to run at the same track where *her runners* were training with her husband, Eddie, who was also a world-class runner trying to transition from competing to coaching. One of the Kenyan runners asked her, "Are we in a concentration camp? Why can't a famous runner like Henry visit us?" Around this time, I confronted Hellebuyck about her stealing from her athletes. She said she wasn't stealing from them since she had paid the KAAA $1,000 per year per runner to have rights to the careers of each of these Kenyan runners. She treated her athletes like heads of livestock, and, like livestock, their future plans and desires were frivolous to her. She was only interested in how these athletes could become the best commodities they could be so as to make her the quickest and easiest financial profit.

However much Hellebuyck wanted to keep me away from her runners, she wanted even more to take advantage of me and find a way to squeeze some money out of my running fame. In the fall of 1997, while I was busy not only volunteering at VHS, but also substitute teaching and working weekends as a skycap, Hellebuyck contacted me about attending an event in Kosovo for which I would receive an appearance fee. When I refused, she became upset and, to spite me, called a sports reporter in Holland to inform him of my years of alcoholism and vagrancy.

Because I turned down Hellebuyck's arrangements to have me travel to Kosovo, I believe she intended to wreck my teaching and coaching career by publicizing the rumors and second-hand accounts she had heard of my past. The Dutch journalist Kees Kooman traveled to Albuquerque and was interviewing my friends, as well as other runners and acquaintances, about me. Kooman approached Coach Jaramillo, whom I had previously discouraged from speaking to out-of-town journalists. However, Jaramillo was ecstatic to have yet another opportunity to see his track program in the limelight—this time in a well-respected European running magazine, *Holland Track and Field News*—and so he went through with the interview. Later, when the story was published, Jaramillo and the principal of VHS, Toby Herrera, brought in someone to translate it from Dutch. When they saw their own names beside accounts of my past troubles, they felt that their jobs could be in jeopardy for hiring me. As a result, after the spring semester, I felt obligated to quit volunteering at VHS.

Hellebuyck may have brought my coaching at VHS to a premature end, however, her misdealings would soon come back to haunt her when a Brazilian runner, who felt exploited by Hellebuyck in various way, including being forced to babysit her children or else suffer severe consequences to his career, sued her. He won his case, which resulted in tremendous financial hardship for Hellebuyck. Still, the story of her corruption never appeared in American papers, only in the Brazilian press. This is yet another example of how the American media routinely protects the names and reputations of corrupt White authority figures while seeking out and exaggerating the problems and misdeeds of minorities lacking power or influence.

Nonetheless, many people still wonder why foreign athletes don't seek legal action against corrupt agents like Hellebuyck. What many people don't understand is that the foreign athletes who don't report mismanagement by agents and coaches to the media or the authorities are terrified of the consequences of doing so, most notably of being deported or falsely accused of a crime. I felt this way when Coach Chaplin either wanted something from me or wanted to keep me from publicizing his corrupt actions toward me. To get me to submit to his wishes, he would often threaten to ship me back to Africa if I didn't keep my mouth shut and do as he told me.

In the summer of 2000, I applied for a full-time teaching position at Jemez Valley High School (JVHS), and Jane Duran, the director of the school district to which I was applying, told me she was interested in hiring me pending a criminal background check. When the background check returned, Duran told me that my New Jersey case had not been closed and that I should talk to my lawyer to check on the outcome of the case. This was a shock to me since I had already received a cash settlement in a lawsuit I had brought against New Jersey for being wrongly imprisoned.

    I contacted my lawyer in the case, Merrill Rubin, and told him I needed verification that my case was closed and that I had no criminal record. Rubin gave me a hard time, telling me that my file was thick and that going through it would be too time intensive for him to get to it anytime soon. I told him I would be willing to pay him, and he said he would think about it. He had better think about it quickly, I told him, since the school year started in two weeks, and I needed to receive my clearance before that in order to sign my contract before the start of the semester or else the job offer from Duran would be void. Duran, sympathizing with my frustrations with my lawyer, decided to give Rubin a call. However, he gave her the runaround too. She told me that she had had similar experiences with lawyers who wouldn't complete even the smallest task for a former client unless that client paid an exorbitant fee. Still, Duran said that, regardless of my lawyer's obstinacy, she had to have proof that the New Jersey case had been resolved before the beginning of the school year on August 15.

It just so happened that while my troubles with Rubin were transpiring, two journalists had contacted me. One was interested in writing a book about my life, and the other wanted to write a feature article on me for *Los Angeles Magazine*. The journalists were interested in my New Jersey lawsuit, and so they contacted Rubin to clarify how the case had ended up. As soon as Rubin realized my case might receive media attention, he became incredibly cooperative and accommodating, telling me that he would have a certificate of clearance faxed to Duran in 24 to 48 hours.

Though the two reporters interested in my story uncovered Rubin's misdealings, neither wrote critically of him. It was the same old journalistic paradigm I had become accustomed to: no reporter will dare speak badly of an authority figure who is White. I began to further reflect on my dealings with Rubin. In my case of mistaken identity, had I been White, I bet I would have received a settlement upwards of a million dollars. However, as a Kenyan, not only did I get a paltry settlement, but I couldn't even get my lawyer to complete the case. He simply left it hanging for a dozen years.

Chapter XXIX
Dream Realized

In August of 2000, I was hired as a full-time special education teacher at Jemez Valley High School (JVHS), a public school on the Jemez Pueblo Indian Reservation. I was drawn to teaching special education students since I learned to speak English as a second language as an adult, which made me empathetic with these students' educational struggles. Beyond this, I felt a special affinity to the Native American students at JVHS as I also came from a tribal culture. Since Jemez Pueblo was 120-miles roundtrip from my Albuquerque residence, I moved to Rio Rancho, a suburb northwest of Albuquerque, to cut down my commute.

Before my first day of teaching, Gerald Snider, the principal of JVHS, offered me a contract to instruct ninth through twelfth grade special education students in mathematics, a subject I felt suitably qualified to teach. However, before I headed into teach on my first day of class, I was told that I would have to teach English and social studies instead. The decision to have me teach subjects outside of my field of expertise brought me a great deal of anxiety as I wondered how a foreigner like me, who had a heavy accent and was himself still learning to master the English language, could be taken seriously by students in English or any other subject in the humanities such as social studies.

Sensing my anxiety, Snider tried to reassure me, saying that the only qualification a good teacher really needs is common sense and that he and the other administrators would be there to help me every step of the way. Still, I worried and questioned my credentials. I wondered, "How could students progress in English class when the teacher himself is still learning to speak, read, and write effectively in English?"

From day one, when the classroom of 15 students realized that they had a foreigner with a heavy accent and only passable communication skills in English as a teacher, they pushed my buttons in every way as an attempt to get me to quit. I was stunned at how disrespectful my students could be to me as they often commanded me to do things, sometimes even scolding me, and frequently insulting me in various ways. Apparently, their misbehavior had succeeded in chasing a series of previous special education instructors out of town. However, I made it clear to them from the beginning that quitting was not an option for me. I told the class, "I know you keep pushing me to see if I will quit, but you should know that I never quit any race I ever ran." Soon, the students began to realize there was something different about me. After acting especially hostile to me during one class and failing to make me lose my temper, the class looked at me with puzzled expressions, and one student turned to the rest of the class and asked, "How come this one never gets sick of us and doesn't give up like the other teachers?"

While teaching at JVHS, I was also volunteering as an assistant coach for the school's cross-country team. I began to wonder whether Snider—who was an amateur runner and former basketball coach at Albuquerque's Valley High School, where he led a long-shot squad to a state championship before deciding to go into administration—only employed me so that I could help the JVHS cross-country program gain greater notoriety. After employing the training routine I had planned for them, JVHS claimed a state cross-country championship in the fall of 2000.

I will be the first to admit that my first semester of teaching was a disaster. I didn't know how to write a lesson plan, and, when I tried to talk to the special educational director or the principal, they were dismissive of me, saying things to the effect of, "You got the job, and now it's your business." At one point during the semester, my students started to openly protest my lack of qualifications and walked out of my classroom, taking their complaints directly to the special education director, who sent the students on a beeline to the principal's office, where Snider asked the students to write a description of how they wanted me to teach them. When I walked by the principal's office, the students were grouping up trying to write a lesson plan. Some of the students were demanding I be fired because I was teaching English without even being able to speak it well. I sincerely empathized with my students and their complaints, and I wondered to myself why they hadn't simply let me teach the subject I was qualified to teach. I felt a deep sense of concern for the quality of my students' education combined with my own self-pity for inheriting an English class without having a firm grasp on the language.

Still, no matter how disorganized I was in the classroom that first semester, my students realized that, despite how poorly qualified I was to teach English, I did deeply care about them and their education. Before winter break, I threw a party for my class, which made one of my students smile for the first time all semester. "Next semester, you will make a lesson plan, won't you?" she asked. I said I was already beginning to learn how to better prepare for my classes. In my second semester, I began to understand the nuances of teaching, and everything started running much more smoothly for me in the classroom. My English had improved dramatically from the practice of formally speaking in front of the class each day, and my students began to sympathize with the situation I was put in as a teacher. Beyond this, they also began to sense that I was one of their greatest advocates among the faculty.

During my experience at JVHS, I came to understand that my students were being shortchanged by the American school system in more ways than one. First of all, they were students from an ethnic minority, and, from my experiences coaching and teaching in the United States, I had come to realize that the educational facilities, as well as the qualifications of teachers, in low-income areas with large minority populations are generally poor. Of all the minorities who are failed by the education system in the United States, Native American students attending schools on reservations are the most disadvantaged in my opinion. Teaching and living on the reservation is so dreaded by most teachers that government programs are forced to lure even unqualified individuals to teach there. The government offers programs in which most anyone with a college degree—regardless of what subject the degree is in and despite a lack of teaching certificate—can receive an emergency license to teach on a reservation school *and*, as an added bonus, even qualify to have student loan debts forgiven to help repay the "sacrifice."

One person told me that once the few qualified teachers in the area are employed, JVHS would take practically anyone off the street with a college degree to teach virtually any subject, regardless of whether or not the person was qualified to teach it. My students, having special education needs, were doubly disadvantaged as it seemed the least qualified teachers of the generally poorly qualified teaching staff at JVHS were assigned special education classes. The United States does not value or compensate teachers to attract qualified and bright individuals to pursue teaching careers. As a result, the most qualified teachers settle at the most affluent schools, leaving the students who need the best teachers—those disadvantaged due to socioeconomic conditions or learning disabilities—with the least qualified and prepared ones.

After my contract at JVHS was up, my interest in and advocacy for both special education and Native American students made me pursue a teaching position at another reservation school, though this time I insisted on teaching a subject for which I was qualified. I found myself at Laguna-Acoma Middle and High School. Laguna was a 125-mile roundtrip commute from my house in Rio Rancho, and, to get my daily run in, I had to get up at 4:00 AM in order to be able to arrive at school before the first bell rang. During this time, I was also taking six hours of evening classes per semester and working part-time at the airport as a skycap. My skycap job was needed to help me pay for my evening classes without depleting the money I routinely sent home to my family in Kenya.

When the pressures of the graduate degree I am still pursuing became too intense to allow me to teach full-time, I decided to return to substitute teaching closer to home in Albuquerque, which would enable me to focus more intensely on my studies. I intend to finish my master's degree in education at UNM sometime in the next 18 months. Despite all my running records and accomplishments, I would consider finishing my graduate degree and receiving a full-time teaching position in special education for Albuquerque Public Schools to be my greatest milestone, since the satisfaction I receive from teaching rivals the joy I got from my running victories. I can feel myself closing in on my greatest achievement, and I'm pushing harder toward the finish.

AFTERWORD

This morning, as I head out for my daily run along the trails near Tramway Boulevard beneath Albuquerque's foothills, I realize that it's been more than a quarter century since the 1980 boycott—the difficult time that signaled the beginning of the most trying years of my life. Usually, my morning run lifts my spirits and takes me far away from those depressing times. However, this morning, my run makes me remember training on these same trails that late summer of 1980, when depression settled over me as politics once again interfered with my ability to compete in the Olympics.

Continuing on my run, these painful memories begin to dissipate as I focus on my current training goals, my teaching aspirations, and my responsibilities to my family in Kenya. Last night, I spoke on my cell phone to my grandmother, Kobotkimisik, who is 116, and she was excited to learn that her name is in this book I'm finishing. This reminds me—this afternoon I'd better not forget to wire the $50 I promised her!

The summer of 2006 has been the rainiest season in Albuquerque's modern history, making the wild grasses grow tall. When I trained here in the early 1980s, Albuquerque was in the middle of a severe drought, and it was dusty and dry beneath the Sandia Mountains. There were few houses and no businesses near Tramway Boulevard, which had not yet been paved. That year, as I ran along the foothill trails, the heat rose to 110 degrees, and the rattlesnakes were everywhere! Every morning on my run, when I least expected, a rattlesnake would coil in front or at the side of my path and make its noise like a fire crackling. I would jump over it and, filled with adrenaline, sprint forward dozens of meters. Inevitably, just as my heart would start to beat normally, there would be another rattler, a longer one, coiled in my path, the sight of which sent me hightailing it back to my apartment with my heart seemingly beating outside of my chest on more than one occasion.

Today, along Tramway, on the bike path that leads to the foothills or along the foothills' rocky terrain, there are no more rattlesnakes. Jackrabbits are the only animals I see besides doves, small songbirds, kestrels, and the occasional hawk or vulture overhead. Near the end of my run, I whisper to myself, "Running is the light to my life." I have come to the end of the tunnel, which marks the transition from the tarmac to dirt trail. By this time, I am on a different path. I no longer relive the frustrations of the '76 or '80 Olympic boycotts or the life troubles that followed. Suddenly, I realize I have been able to overcome my alcoholism and long depression by keeping running.

HENRY RONO is currently training to break the world record in the mile for men 55 and over. To track Henry's pursuit of the record, and to keep up with his other endeavors, please visit http://www.team-rono.com.

CPSIA information can be obtained at www.ICGtesting.com
Printed in the USA
LVOW082324140312

273119LV00001B/30/P